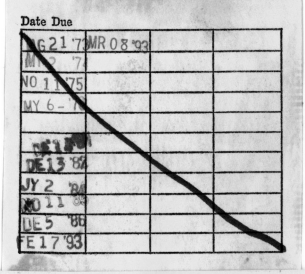

An Introduction to
Supreme Court Decision Making

CHANDLER PUBLICATIONS IN
POLITICAL SCIENCE

Victor Jones, *Editor*

An Introduction to
Supreme Court
Decision Making

Revised and Enlarged Edition

Harold J. Spaeth

Michigan State University

CHANDLER PUBLISHING COMPANY
An **Intext** Publisher
SAN FRANCISCO · SCRANTON · LONDON · TORONTO

Library of Congress Cataloging in Publication Data

Spaeth, Harold J
  An Introduction to Supreme Court decision making.

          (Chandler publications in political science)
          Bibliography: p.
  1. U. S. Supreme Court. 2. Judicial process—U. S. I. Title. II. Title: Supreme
Court decision making.
KF8748.S54 1972   347′.73′265   78-171594
ISBN 0-8102-0440-1

BOOK DESIGN *R. Keith Richardson*

To my mother,

Julia Quinlan Spaeth

Contents

Foreword

A number of landmark decisions have been made by the Supreme Court since the first edition of this book appeared seven years ago. But this alone does not justify a second edition, for the purpose of the book remains the same: "to present a self-contained explanation of Supreme Court decision making, and to do so within a context which emphasizes the political features of Supreme Court activity."

What warrants this second edition are the theoretical advances which have been made since 1965. The rudiments of a theory of Supreme Court decision making that appear herein result from a number of factors: increased interaction among social scientists across disciplinary boundaries, a greater concern for methodological rigor and the reliability of measuring instruments, the collection of sufficient data to test hypotheses and build theories, and an increase in financial support to social scientists from governmental and private funding agencies in the last half of the 1960s. As a result, a number of fields within the various social science disciplines have begun a slow—but hopefully steady—advance toward scientific maturity.

My dependence upon others for the material contained in this edition is extensive. Although data collected for earlier periods in the Court's history have not been directly utilized herein, those gathered by Donald C. Leavitt of Wayne State University, Mary R. Mattingly of Texas A. & I. University, and Peter G. Renstrom of Western Michigan University have provided a comparative basis from which I have been able to analyze Supreme Court decision making of the last fifteen to twenty years. Scott B. Guthery of Bell Telephone Laboratories, David J. Peterson of the Capitol Campus of Pennsylvania State University, and Charles B. Poland of I.B.M. have patiently shared their methodological expertise with me. Collaboration on other research with Drs. Guthery and Peterson has been especially beneficial.

From Douglas R. Parker of Cleveland State University and my colleague, David W. Rohde, I have learned much about the nature of theory. These two individuals read and commented upon the manuscript in their invariably insightful fashion. Doug Parker, especially, kept me from numerous errors of fact and interpretation, and his editorial skills greatly improved the clarity and readability of the manuscript. Jean Daulton Spaeth, my wife, and Susan Kerr Rutkowski read the manuscript from a nonprofessional perspective, with the result that the number of gratuitous statements has been markedly reduced from what the manuscript otherwise would have contained.

A special debt is owed Maxim Goode of R-Squared, Inc. of Los Angeles. As an outstanding journalist and recognized expert in the use of computer technology to predict and explain the outcome of events in a domain other than the political, his encouragement of my efforts scientifically to predict and explain the outcome of Supreme Court decisions has been most gratifying. Much of the data contained herein has appeared in altered form in materials published by R-Squared.

Lessening the costs of computer–dependent research has been the financial assistance granted me by the National Institute of Mental Health and the cooperation provided by Charles F. Wrigley, director of the Michigan State University Computer Institute for Social Science Research, and others previously or currently associated with the Computer Institute—especially Scott B. Guthery, Leighton A. Price, and Stuart Thomas, Jr. In this regard, I also acknowledge the cooperation and assistance of my department chairman, Charles Press.

Lastly, I owe thanks to the more than 1800 students who have listened and reacted to my lectures on The American Judicial Process during the past seven years. It is they who have made me aware of the intimate relationship between teaching and research.

Harold J. Spaeth

Michigan State University

An Introduction to
Supreme Court Decision Making

The Functions of the Judiciary in the American Political System

In broadest compass, the functions of courts may be described as three-fold: administration of the laws, conflict resolution, and policy making.

The first of these functions pertains to the administration of those laws by which a society, through its law makers, defines certain actions to be criminal. The most general explanation for the promulgation of such laws is that man is a creature of habit who is psychologically incapable of functioning in an overly dynamic environment. To some extent and within certain degrees of freedom, an individual must be able to demand from others certain regularities of behavior, and to accord to others the expectation that he too will behave predictably. Consequently, for the purpose of securing regularity in important kinds of interpersonal behavior, societies enact laws, the violation of which is a crime.

The second of the functions performed by courts, conflict resolution, pertains to the settlement of private disputes. In addition to being a creature of habit, man is also motivated by self-interest. Being so motivated, he comes into conflict with others. Conflicts generated by an individual's self-interest often are sufficiently personal that society does not regulate them by means of criminal law. But to the affected individual, such conflicts are a matter of great concern, so much so that his personal well-being may be adversely affected. Consequently, society provides a mechanism —civil law—for the resolution of such private disputes in a socially acceptable manner.

In making provision for the settlement of private disputes,

American society provides three distinguishable services:[1] (1) the provision of a forum (the court) and a set of procedures and remedies by which the conflict may be resolved; (2) the legitimization of private settlements whereby private actions may be legalized, *e.g.*, the termination of a marriage, the adoption of a child, or the execution of a will; (3) the use of governmental power by citizens for private purposes, *e.g.*, the granting of a writ of injunction or mandamus, the ejection of a tenant, or the garnishment of a person's salary.

These first two functions—administration of the criminal law and conflict resolution through the civil law—often lead to the third major function of the courts: policy making. In the realm of the administration of the criminal law, this can happen, for example, when one of the provisions of the Bill of Rights is called into question. In the realm of conflict resolution through the civil law, it can happen when the outcome of a "private" dispute has widespread implications for, or impact on, society as a whole—for example, labor-management relations and governmental regulation of business.

Policy making is rather distinctive to the United States. This policy-making function pertains to the fact that courts are called upon to resolve basic public policy issues. Unlike administration of the laws and conflict resolution, however, not all American courts perform a policy-making function equally. Paramount is the United States Supreme Court because it is located at the apex of the hierarchy of courts and because it is empowered to authoritatively adjudicate issues arising out of the Constitution, Acts of Congress, and United States treaties. On issues not covered by the federal Constitution or laws, state supreme courts function as the paramount judicial policy makers.

Because judicial policy making is both central and distinctive to the operation of the American judiciary, an explanation of the reasons for its existence is in order.

Guiding the development of the American political system was

---

[1]Herbert Jacob, *Debtors in Court: The Consumption of Governmental Services* (Chicago: Rand-McNally, 1969), pp. 16–17. The first two of these three services are discussed in *Boddie* v. *Connecticut*, 401 U.S. 371 (1971).

the concept of a fundamental law. The religiously motivated founding of most of the colonies north of Virginia resulted in governments that were based upon sectarian interpretations of the Bible or natural law. With the formation of the United States and the inclusion within a single governmental system of a diversity of viewpoints concerning the word of God and the dictates of nature, the need for a less parochial fundamental law became apparent. The solution, of course, was the enshrinement of the Constitution as American society's secular substitute for Holy Writ.

A second reason for judicial policy making is the fear of centralized governmental power. In drafting the Constitution, the Framers were mindful of their experiences as subjects of Great Britain. Opposition to British governmental policies had caused the Revolutionary War. In addition, concurrent with the Revolution had occurred an internal struggle for political dominance between the upper and lower classes within the various newly formed American states. The result at the national level was a government which neither the "haves" nor the "have nots" were capable of using as a vehicle to subjugate the other. The view that that government is best which governs least became an accepted article of faith for most Americans. Sentiments supportive of states' rights and local self-government, plus the fact that many Americans lived on the frontier, beyond the pale of effective governmental authority, gave added vitality to this sentiment.

The geographical spread of the United States, the lack of easy means of transportation and communication, and the fear of centralized government caused the Framers to establish a federal system of government—one in which the powers which government was authorized to exercise were divided between the national level and the states. The Constitutional provisions pertaining to the division of power between the national government and the states are unclear. What powers the national government may exercise, those that are the province of the states, and those that both may utilize have provoked a steady stream of litigation since the adoption of the Constitution. Responsible for final adjudication of such questions is the Supreme Court. In this aspect of its policy-making function—determining the relative power of one level vis-à-vis the other and the resultant degree of centralization/decentralization that is to prevail—the Supreme Court is aptly described as the umpire of the federal system. An excellent example was the attempt by Congress in 1970 to lower the voting age to eighteen. The Court held that Congress has the power to do so for elections to federal offices, but not for those to state and local offices (*Oregon* v. *Mitchell*, 400 U.S. 112).

To further ensure that the activities of the national government did not exceed the limits specified in the fundamental law, three autonomous branches were established which were roughly parallel to the classic typology of governmental functions: executive, legislative, and judicial. This "separation of powers" is accomplished by the constitutional provision that prohibits an official in one branch from simultaneously holding office in another. To preserve the autonomy of each branch, the Framers gave to each the authority to exercise powers that properly pertain to the others, thereby enabling any given branch to "check and balance" the activities of the others. Thus, Congress must approve major executive appointments; the President may veto congressional legislation; and the judiciary determines the constitutionality of legislative and executive action.

Separation of powers has also enabled judges to be viewed as distinct from other political actors. If judges were not substantially autonomous of the President and Congress, their ability to present themselves as objective and impartial decision makers would be much more difficult. Without such autonomy, the public might likely tar judges with the same brush that is applied to politicians and bureaucrats generally—that politics is a dirty business and that only persons of minimal abilities work for government. And, consequently, that judges should no more be viewed as guardians of the Constitution and protectors of people and their rights than are other political actors.

Because of separation of powers, conflict is institutionalized between the President and Congress. Each is forced to compete with the other for power. The judiciary is able to remain aloof from this competition because it does not employ coercive economic or physical sanctions to effectuate its decisions. Hence, when the President and Congress disagree over policies, the Supreme Court is able to tip the balance of power. One of the more dramatic examples from the past was the Steel Seizure Case of 1952 (*Youngstown Sheet and Tube Co.* v. *Sawyer,* 343 U.S. 579), in which the Court sided with Congress in voiding President Truman's order that the government operate the steel mills to avert a nationwide strike that would adversely affect the Korean War effort.

Not all commentators and judges admit the fact of judicial policy making. Indeed, before 1930, any suggestion that courts in general or the Supreme Court in particular did anything other than administer laws and resolve conflicts was likely to be met with denunciation. The most fundamental reason for denying the existence of judicial policy making is the psychological need of individuals for stability and security, for some contact with the invariant, in the flux of life. It was precisely because of this psychological need that American society institutionalized the notion of fundamental law with the adoption of the Constitution. Other areas of human activity—the social, economic, cultural, and religious, during all but the most recent years of American history—have not been amenable to effective human direction and control. From the colonial period to the present, individual Americans experienced drastic fluctuations in life style, status, and economic well-being. The recession of the frontier as the nation expanded across the continent; the industrial and technological revolutions, whereby a nation of small farm owners was transformed into urbanized employees; the impact of immigration, urbanization, mass transportation, and communication; all precluded the establishment of fixed and stable social, economic, cultural, and religious systems. Only the political sphere provided an opportunity for stability. In looking to the courts for stability and security, wish-fulfillment caused judges to be viewed as objective, impartial, and dispassionate decision makers who nondiscretionally applied the law and resolved disputes in accordance with the provisions of the fundamental, unchanging law—the Constitution. An irreverent attack upon this point of view, dating from the early days of the New Deal, was republished some years ago by one of my former colleagues:

Song of the Supreme Court[2]

We're nine judicial gentlemen who shun the common herd,
Nine official mental men who speak the final word.
We do not issue postage stamps or face the microphones,
Or osculate with infants, or preside at corner-stones.
But we're the court of last resort in litigation legal.
(See: Case of Brooklyn Chicken *versus* Washington Blue Eagle.)
We never heed the demagogues, their millions and their minions,
But use *this* handy yardstick when in doubt about opinions:

Chorus

If it's In The Constitution, it's the law,
For The Constitution hasn't got a flaw.
If it's In The Constitution, it's okay,
Whether yesterday, tomorrow, or today—
Hooray!

If it's In The Constitution, it must stay!
Like oysters in our cloisters, we avoid the storm and strife.
Some President appoints us, and we're put away for life.
When Congress passes laws that lack historical foundation,
We hasten from a huddle and reverse the legislation.
The sainted Constitution, that great document for students,
Provides an airtight alibi for all our jurisprudence.
So don't blame us if now and then we seem to act like bounders;
Blame Hamilton and Franklin and the patriotic founders.

Chorus

If it's In The Constitution, it's the law, *etc.*

---

[2]By Arthur L. Lippmann, in the original *Life Magazine*, 102 (August 1935), 7; reprinted in Glendon Schubert, *Constitutional Politics* (New York: Holt, Rinehart and Winston, 1960), pp. 11–12.

Two additional reasons why defenders of dispassionate judicial decision making have denied courts' possession of a policy-making function are: judges lack coercive capabilities; consequently, they are theoretically vulnerable to sanctions from other decision makers in the political system, such as loss of jurisdiction, a change in the number of judges, and if elected the failure of re-election. The second reason is that when a court makes policy it in no way performs any activity that is not present when it simply administers the laws or resolves conflicts. This absence of distinguishable activity allows those who wish to do so to deny that judges perform any function other than administration of the laws and conflict resolution.

In performing its functions, especially that of policy making, the Supreme Court has fundamentally shaped the character of American government and politics. The Court's decisions have affected not only judges, lawyers, and litigants but, more important, they have significantly influenced the character and direction of American politics and society. From a strictly legal point of view the decision in a particular case can be said to affect only the parties directly involved. But such a view is not only narrow; it also ignores the role which the Supreme Court has played since the time of Chief Justice John Marshall at the beginning of the nineteenth century. Admittedly, this role is one which appears restricted to the legal order. But from a broader perspective one can see that the decision making of the Supreme Court has shaped as well as reflected our political life, social structure, economic system, cultural heritage, and religious traditions—in short, all that goes to make up "the American way of life." Thus it may fairly be said that the Supreme Court has shaped and directed the course of American society at least as much—and arguably more than—any other unit in the American governmental system.

2

The Appointment of the Justices

Between September 26, 1789 and January 1, 1971, ninety-nine persons, all male, had served on the United States Supreme Court. Each of these persons, compatibly with the provisions of the Constitution, had been nominated by the President and confirmed by a majority vote of the Senate. An additional seven persons, having been nominated and confirmed, declined to accept appointment. Five of these instances occurred between 1789 and 1811; the other two in 1837 and 1882.

An additional twenty-seven persons were nominated by the President but failed of confirmation. Three of these, however, were subsequently confirmed. Of the remaining twenty-four, fourteen failed of confirmation in the thirty years between 1844 and 1874. Only three nominees failed before 1844, and only one nominee in the years from 1895 through 1967.

Analysis of the twenty-four situations in which a nominee failed to be confirmed indicates that three distinguishable sets of circumstances may explain the outcome: lack of nominee qualifications, conflict between the President and a majority of the senators, and the lame-duck status of the President. The last of these pertains to the last months of a President's term of office when he is about to be replaced by his successor.

Seven nominees by Presidents in a lame-duck status have been rejected. The record for a single President was Fillmore, who had three nominees rejected in 1852–1853. The most recent example of the lame-duck phenomenon occurred in the Spring of 1968 when President Johnson's nomination of Abe Fortas for promotion to the chief justiceship and that of Homer Thornberry as associate justice were not acted upon by the Senate. Of the thirteen persons failing of confirmation because of political differences between the President and Senate, five failed during the post-Civil War period, three of whom were nominated by Grant, two by Cleveland. The record for a single President was Tyler, who had four nominees rejected on this basis in 1844–1845. Lack of qualifications explains the crucial votes in four instances: John Rutledge in 1795; Alexander Wolcott in 1811; Clement Haynsworth in 1969; and G. Harrold Carswell, five months later, in 1970.

Prior to 1970, two successive nominees of a single President had not failed to be confirmed since 1894. Haynsworth was rejected because of conflict of interest, the same reason that had forced Justice Fortas to resign six months earlier. (Fortas thus became the first member of the Court in history to resign because of public pressure.) President Nixon's nomination of Carswell was rejected because of his alleged mediocrity and reputed racist values.[3] In the Carswell vote, 30% of the Senators from the President's party voted against confirmation, while 40% did so on the Haynsworth vote.

As a general rule, Presidents desire to appoint persons to the Court who reflect their own personal policy preferences. Normally, this means that the nominee will be a member of the President's party. There have been exceptions, however. President Taft equally divided his six nominations between Republicans and Democrats. Taft, incidentally, saw more of his nominees confirmed than any other Presidents except Washington, Jackson, and F. D. Roosevelt. Taft, moreover, served but a single term as President.

In seeking to appoint persons who share their public policy views, Presidents have occasionally guessed wrongly. To mention but two examples: the liberal Wilson appointed James McReynolds, whom many view as the most reactionary justice ever to sit on the Court. And it is likely that Eisenhower was less than happy with many of the decisions of his Chief Justice, Earl Warren.

---

[3] For the story of Carswell's nomination and his rejection by the Senate, see Richard Harris, *Decision* (New York: Dutton, 1971).

Apart from the unwritten rule that the nominee be a lawyer and an American citizen, Presidents are free to nominate whom they wish. A President may choose to consider such factors as geographical and religious representation, the mood of the Senate, and sundry other political considerations in making a nomination, but he is under no compulsion to do so.

The high status of the Court and the prestige that comes from membership thereon correlates highly with the backgrounds of the persons who have occupied positions on the nation's highest tribunal. The great majority have been white Anglo-Saxon Protestants, from middle and upper-income families. "Not only were [they] from families in comfortable economic circumstances but were chosen overwhelmingly from the socially prestigeful and politically influential gentry class in the . . . eighteenth and early nineteenth century or the professionalized upper-middle class thereafter."[4] Only two justices, George Shiras and Harry Blackmun were not politically active. All practiced law at some stage of their careers. No person of Italian or Slavic ancestry has sat on the Court. The only black, Thurgood Marshall, was appointed in 1967. Six Catholics have served, including two chief justices, Taney and Edward White. Justice Brennan is the most recent Catholic to sit. Five Jews have also served; the first was Brandeis in 1916; most recently, Arthur Goldberg sat from 1962 to 1965; Abe Fortas from 1965 to 1969. Religiously, most of the other justices have been members of high status Protestant denominations: Episcopalian, Presbyterian, Congregationalist, and Unitarian.

Once appointed, a justice, according to the Constitution, serves for life "during good behavior". No member of the Court has ever been successfully impeached. The closest a member of the Court came was Samuel Chase in 1804. The House of Representatives did vote to impeach him, but he was acquitted by the Senate. On the other hand, impeachment resolutions have been introduced against numerous justices. But with the exception of Chase, the House has never approved such a resolution. The most

---

[4]John R. Schmidhauser, *The Supreme Court: Its Politics, Personalities, and Procedures* (New York: Holt, Rinehart and Winston, 1960), p. 32.

recent attempt to impeach a member of the Court occurred in the Spring of 1970, when fifty-two conservative Republicans and an equal number of Democrats, mostly Southerners, introduced a resolution calling for Justice Douglas' impeachment. This was not the first time such a resolution had been introduced against Douglas. His three divorces, off-the-bench writings, and liberal voting record had made him a target of conservatives for twenty years. The effort failed in December 1970 when the subcommittee to which the resolution was referred concluded that no grounds for Douglas' impeachment existed.[5]

---

[5]Triggering this impeachment effort was the appearance of excerpts from Douglas' book, *Points of Rebellion* (New York: Random House, 1970), in *Evergreen Review* 14 (1970), 41–43. The excerpts appeared immediately after a seven-page display of nude photos of oral-genital sex.

A more detailed study of the appointment of the justices may be found in Robert Scigliano, *The Supreme Court and the Presidency* (New York: Free Press, 1971), chaps. 4–5.

3

The Utility of the Case Approach

The medium through which the Court effectuates its role in the American governmental system is the cases that embody the controversies it is called upon to decide. Hence, anyone who wishes to know and comprehend the impact of the Supreme Court on the American governmental system is well advised to study these cases themselves.

The case approach is useful in several respects. In the first place, the case approach provides the student of the Court with the original document, the official record. He is not dependent for his knowledge upon a commentator's summary or interpretation, but can study the facts at firsthand.

Second, the opinions of the Court constitute an intelligible and accessible record of the major political issues that have convulsed American society over the course of its history: federalism, separation of powers, the regulation of the economy, revenue policy, and civil rights and liberties. That the major issues of American politics readily make their way into the courts is as true today as at any time in our constitutional history; *e.g.*, the Pentagon Papers Case[6] Quite clearly, these issues are not merely political in that they concern relationships between the rulers and the ruled, but pertain to the social, economic, cultural, and ethical aspects of life as well. Thus, for example, a case involving Bible reading in the public schools necessarily has effects in the sphere of religion. A case concerned with freedom of the press may well involve moral questions of obscenity and pornography. A case involving business or labor may vitally affect the operation of the economic system. A civil rights action, a poverty law case, or one

---

[6] *United States* v. *New York Times* 403 U.S. 713 (1971).

pertaining to the draft will necessarily have interconnected social, economic, ethical, and cultural repercussions. And so on.

Third, in considerations of the major issues, the opinions of the Court frequently reveal a clash of views. It is not unusual for the Court to disagree in important cases. The justices are free to dissent or concur, and these opinions present alternative ways of resolving the policy question at issue.[7] The study of these minority views allows the student to appraise conflicting viewpoints contained in the opinions.

Finally, the case approach is equally useful whether the focus of study is traditional or behavioral. Those of a traditional orientation have, of course, long employed the case approach in their concern with legal argumentation, adherence to precedent, and the evolution of legal and constitutional principles. Behavioralists similarly have found the case approach germane to their focus upon the sociological, psychological, and political aspects of judicial behavior and decision making.

Since the decisions of the Supreme Court encompass the breadth of American politics, the utility of the case approach is broadly relevant. Virtually every aspect of American government and politics has its pertinent Supreme Court decisions. Some aspects have been decisively affected by judicial decisions. For instance, in the area of the First Amendment freedoms and the rights of persons accused of crime, the Court's decisions virtually determine the character and scope of these rights and liberties, independent of action taken by Congress, the President, or the state governments. Similarly, in the area of civil rights, the Court's voice is crucial.

The Court has the authority to specify the scope and limits not only of its own power along with that of the federal judiciary, e.g., *Marbury* v. *Madison*, 1 Cr. 137 (1803), *Ex parte McCardle*, 7 Wall. 506 (1869), *Baker* v. *Carr*, 369 U.S. 186 (1962); but also the limits of Congressional power, e.g., *Wickard* v. *Filburn*, 317 U.S. 111 (1942), *Watkins* v. *United States*, 354 U.S. 178 (1957), *Powell* v. *McCormack* 395 U.S. 486 (1969), *Oregon* v. *Mitchell*, 400 U.S. 112

---

[7]An extreme example was the Pentagon Papers Case, 403 U.S. 713 (1971), in which each of the nine justices wrote an opinion.

(1970); those of the President, e.g., *Humphrey's Executor* v. *United States*, 295 U.S. 602 (1935), *Korematsu* v. *United States*, 323 U.S. 214 (1944); and the federal administrative agencies, e.g., *NLRB* v. *Jones & Laughlin Steel Corp.*, 301 U.S. 1 (1937), *Gutknecht* v. *United States*, 396 U.S. 295 (1970).

This is not to say that all public policy issues are susceptible to effective resolution by the Supreme or other courts. A court may lack jurisdiction to hear a given issue or the relevant legislation may be inadequate to allow the courts to remedy an admittedly inequitable situation. In a number of states, for example, a divorce can be granted, even when both partners desire it, only upon a showing that one of the partners is guilty of wrongdoing. The judiciary's effectiveness may also be lessened because the issue in question is one that evokes deeply rooted and intense feelings. Thus, the lack of compliance that followed upon the Supreme Court's decision relating to released time and school prayers,[8] the well-publicized hostility to court ordered school desegregation,[9] and the use of the courts to try radical political dissenters during periods of national unrest. The most significant recent example of such trials was that of the "Chicago Seven."[10]

---

[8]On released-time programs of religious instruction, see *McCollum* v. *Board of Education*, 333 U.S. 203 (1948); *Zorach* v. *Clauson*, 343 U.S. 306 (1952); Gordon Patric, "The Impact of a Court Decision: Aftermath of the McCollum Case," *Journal of Public Law* 6 (1957), 455–464; Frank J. Sorauf, *Zorach* v. *Clauson*: The Impact of a Supreme Court Decision," *American Political Science Review*, 53 (1959), 777–791. On school prayers, see *Engel* v. *Vitale*, 370 U.S. 421 (1962); *Abingdon* v. *Schempp*, 374 U.S. 203 (1963); H. Frank Way, "Survey Research on Judicial Decisions: The Prayer and Bible Reading Cases," *Western Political Quarterly*, 21 (1968), 189–205; William Beaney and N. Edward Beiser, "Prayer and Politics: The Impact of Engel and Schempp on the Political Process," *Journal of Public Law*, 13 (1964), 475–503; Robert Birkby, "The Supreme Court and the Bible Belt: Tennessee Reaction to the Schempp Decision," *Midwest Journal of Political Science*, 10 (1966), 304–319. Also see the Parochiaid Cases: *Lemon* v. *Kurtzman* 401 U.S. 931 (1971); and *Tilton* v. *Richardson*, 401 U.S. 931 (1971).

[9]See J. W. Peltason, *Fifty-Eight Lonely Men: Southern Federal Judges and School Desegregation* (New York: Harcourt, Brace & World, 1961). On compliance generally, see Theodore L. Becker (ed.), *The Impact of Supreme Court Decisions: Empirical Studies* (New York: Oxford University Press, 1969), and Stephen L. Wasby, *The Impact of the United States Supreme Court: Some Perspectives* (Homewood, Ill.: Dorsey, 1970).

[10]Highly critical reports of this trial and its aftermath are found in: Mark L. Levine, *et al* (eds.), *The Tales of Hoffman* (New York: Bantam Books, 1970); *Con-*

For the student of history or political thought, the decisions of the Court punctuate the record of America's growth as a civilization: *Marbury* v. *Madison, Fletcher* v. *Peck, McCulloch* v. *Maryland, Dartmouth College* v. *Woodward, Gibbons* v. *Ogden, Cooley* v. *Board of Wardens, The Slaughter-House Cases, Plessy* v. *Ferguson, Lochner* v. *New York, Adkins* v. *Children's Hospital.* Throughout the nation's history the Court has been intimately involved in determining the actions of government in such matters as transportation, communication, agriculture, banking, industrial enterprise, trade and commerce, labor relations, conditions of employment, taxation and fiscal policy, natural resources, public health, and social welfare. Furthermore, the Court is closely involved with the critical problem of the relationship between the federal government and the states. Indeed, the only area of American governmental policy making with which the Court is not deeply concerned is foreign affairs. But even here, there are decisions which one may read with profit, such as *Youngstown Sheet and Tube Co.* v. *Sawyer* (the famous Steel Seizure Case), *Missouri* v. *Holland, United States* v. *Curtiss-Wright Export Corp., Aptheker* v. *Secretary of State,* and *United States* v. *New York Times.*[11]

---

tempt (Chicago: Swallow, 1970); J. Anthony Lukas, *The Barnyard Epithet and Other Obscenities* (New York: Harper & Row, 1970). For the Supreme Court's position on disruptive courtroom behavior, see *Illinois* v. *Allen,* 397 U.S. 337 (1970).

[11]343 U.S. 579 (1952), 252 U.S. 416 (1920), 299 U.S. 304 (1936), 378 U.S. 500 (1964), and 403 U.S. 713 (1971).

4

The Jurisdiction of the Supreme Court

The sorts of cases which the Supreme Court is concerned with are described in Article III of the Constitution. Accordingly, the Court's jurisdiction extends to all cases which involve a provision of the Constitution, or a law or treaty of the United States. Cases concerning certain types of litigants also fall within the purview of the Supreme Court: those where the United States is a party, those between two or more states, those between residents of different states, those where a state takes action against residents of another state, and those involving foreign diplomatic personnel. The grant of jurisdiction contained in Article III is sufficiently broad to insure that no policies of major moment are excluded from the Court's inspection.

Although a contrary impression is widespread, the Supreme Court does not exist for the purpose of righting every wrong. The demands upon its time preclude the Court's considering any but the most important policy questions. However, this fact does not mean that the Court is inaccessible to the average citizen; if his case presents important questions which affect many similarly situated individuals, the Court is open to his plea. Indeed, a majority of civil rights and liberties cases are brought by individuals of humble means.

But in either of two circumstances, an important policy issue does not receive Supreme Court consideration. Either no case arose over the issue, or the Court itself refused to consider the matter. On the first point, the Supreme Court, like other federal courts, may not initiate legal action. That is to say, the Court may hear only cases brought to it by persons who are at odds over a matter which involves valuable legal rights. These valuable legal rights must be threatened with imminent abridgement and the dispute must be such that the Court is competent to grant relief. Consequently, and unlike the Presidency, Congress, or the state governments, the judiciary is not a self-starting unit of government. A requisite to any action is the existence of a bona fide case or controversy. While this requirement may occasionally delay the judiciary's involvement in a specific issue, it is rare for an appropriate case not to be forthcoming.

The second reason whereby an important policy issue does not receive the attention of the Supreme Court is of considerably greater moment. Unlike any other American court, the Supreme Court has complete authority to hear or refuse to hear any case brought before it. Technically, the Court must accept those cases which come to it by means of a writ of appeal. These comprise roughly ten per cent of the total number of cases filed with the Court. But although the Court must *accept* cases brought by writ of appeal, it need not necessarily decide them. The device by which the Court avoids deciding an appeal is to rule that the case does not contain an issue of sufficient significance to warrant the Court's attention ("appeal dismissed for want of a substantial federal question") or that the case falls outside the scope of its jurisdiction ("appeal dismissed for want of jurisdiction").

The Court's total control over its dockets, of the cases which it accepts for decision, is useful: this control allows the Court to avoid such issues as it wishes to avoid. Since the Court is by no means immune from adverse public sentiment or the wrath of Congress or the President, discretion is not without value to such a policy-making body. And inasmuch as the Court has little besides its moral authority to support its decisions, lacking as it does direct control over the purse strings or the enforcement agencies of government, the Court not uncommonly avoids deciding, at least temporarily, those issues which it considers not ripe for decision in the context of a particular case or which are at the time laden with too much emotion. Thus, in the furor following the School Desegregation Cases of 1954, the Court avoided passing on the constitutionality of state laws prohibiting interracial marriage, the most sensitive aspect of race relations until 1967, when it unanimously declared such laws unconstitutional in *Loving* v. *Virginia*, 388 U.S. 1.

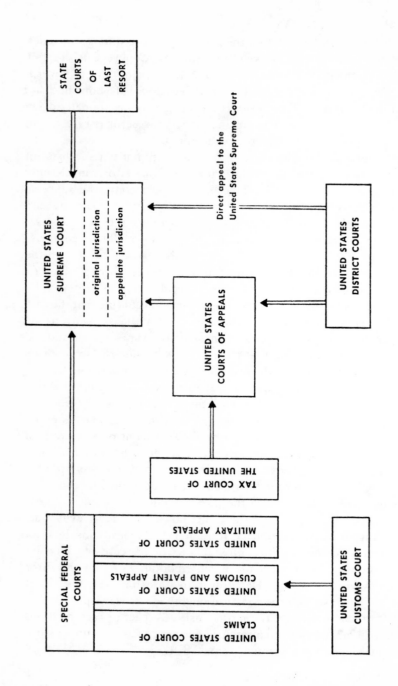

The Supreme Court, the Court of Appeals, and the District Courts are sometimes considered the regular federal courts as distinguished from the special federal courts.

The Supreme Court

The Supreme Court has original jurisdiction over (1) cases concerning ambassadors, ministers, and consuls and over (2) cases where a state is a party.

The Supreme Court has appellate jurisdiction over (1) cases tried or reviewed in the United States Courts of Appeals and the District Courts and over (2) cases tried or reviewed in the highest state courts which raise federal questions—that is, those construing the United States Constitution, Acts of Congress, or treaties with foreign powers.

Extremely few cases arise under the Court's original jurisdiction, and those that do are usually without policy significance. One exception: the eighteen-year-old voting case, *Oregon* v. *Mitchell,* 400 U.S. 112 (1970).

The Courts of Appeals

There are eleven Courts of Appeals, one of which is for the District of Columbia.

The Courts of Appeals have appellate jurisdiction over (1) cases tried in the District Courts; (2) cases heard and decided by the federal regulatory commissions (Interstate Commerce Commission, Federal Communications Commission, National Labor Relations Board, and the like).

The District Courts

There are 91 District Courts: four in United States territories, one in the District of Columbia (these also have jurisdiction over local laws and regulations), and at least one in each state.

The District Courts have original jurisdiction over (1) cases involving the United States Constitution, Acts of Congress, or treaties with foreign powers; (2) suits between residents of different states where the amount in controversy exceeds $10,000; (3) cases of admiralty or maritime jurisdiction; (4) cases where the United States is a party; (5) cases brought by a state against residents of another state; (6) cases between a state, or its residents, and foreign states or citizens; (7) cases between two or more states.

Direct Appeal from the District Courts

The decision of a District Court may be appealed directly to the Supreme Court where (1) a federal law is held unconstitutional; (2) a District Court has made a certain type of decision in a criminal case adverse to the United

States; (3) a civil action is brought by the United States under the antitrust laws, the Interstate Commerce Act, or Title II of the Federal Communications Act; (4) an injunction proceeding is brought to set aside an order of the Interstate Commerce Commission or to restrain enforcement of a state or federal statute on grounds of unconstitutionality.

The Special Federal Courts

The Supreme Court rarely accepts cases for review from the special federal courts.

The Court of Claims hears cases against the United States in other than tort actions. Most cases arise out of public contracts.

The Customs Court reviews appraisals of decisions and Collectors of Customs.

The Court of Customs and Patent Appeals hears appeals from decisions of the Customs Court and the Patent Office.

The Tax Court, formerly the Board of Tax Appeals, is an independent executive agency; it adjudicates controversies involving taxes owed the United States.

The Court of Military Appeals reviews decisions of Courts Martial.

5

The Investigation of
a Supreme Court Case

CASE TITLE AND CITATION

For convenience, Supreme Court cases are referred to by titles which are usually comprised of the names of the principal litigants, the loser of the previous lower-court action versus the winner of that action. Thus, in *United States* v. (for *versus*) *First National Bank & Trust Company of Lexington*, the United States was the losing party in the action before the United States District Court for the Eastern District of Kentucky, which heard the case prior to the Supreme Court's acceptance of the matter. Similarly, in *Mapp* v. *Ohio*, Mapp was the losing party before the Supreme Court of Ohio (the court which heard the case prior to its submission to the United States Supreme Court). Not infrequently, the words "et al." will follow the name of one or other of the litigants, this being the abbreviation of the Latin phrase *et alii*, "and others." It simply indicates that a number of persons, government units, corporations, or other legal entities are jointly engaged in the litigation.

The losing party in the lower-court action, being the party which brings the case to the Court's attention, is referred to in the opinions of the Court as the *plaintiff, petitioner,* or *appellant.* The party against whom action is taken is called the *defendant, respondent,* or *appellee.*

Supreme Court cases are identified not only by case title, but also by citation to one or more of the three publishers who print all of the Court's decisions. In the opinion of the Court in *United States* v. *First National Bank & Trust Company of Lexington,* for example, one of the publishers includes the following statement:

The case, we think, is governed by *Northern Securities Co.* v. *United States*, 193 U.S. 197, 48 L ed 679, 24 S Ct 436 . . .

This passage includes a reference to all three of the published sources of Supreme Court decisions. The "U.S." refers to the *United States Reports*, published by the United States Government Printing Office. "L ed" refers to the *Lawyers' Edition* of the Supreme Court's decisions, published by the Lawyers Co-Operative Publishing Company in Rochester, New York; decisions of the Court handed down since November, 1956, are contained in a second series, cited as "L ed 2d." The final citation, "S Ct," is to the *Supreme Court Reporter*, which is published by the West Publishing Company in St. Paul, Minnesota. The latter two series are published by commercial houses and are less widely used than the *United States Reports*.[12]

Each source reference is preceded by the volume number in which the case may be found, while the number following the publisher's abbreviation specifies the page of the volume where the case begins. Not infrequently, a case citation may include the year in which the case was decided. Thus: *Northern Securities Co.* v. *United States*, 193 U.S. 197 (1904). Most commonly cited is the *United States Reports*, and both of the commercial sources are cross indexed to it. Consequently, even though one has access only to the *Lawyers' Edition* or to the *Supreme Court Reporter*, it is no problem to locate cases therein even though only the citation to the *United States Reports* is at hand.

In reading through opinions of the Court, one runs across frequent references to decisions of the lower federal courts in addition to those of state supreme courts. Decisions of both of the important lower federal courts, the district courts and the courts of appeals decided prior to 1925 are contained in the *Federal Reporter*. These are cited as "Fed." or "F." A second series contains cases decided since 1925 and is cited as "Fed. (2d)" or "F. (2d)." Since 1932, the decisions of the district courts have been

---

[12]Prior to 1875, the *United States Reports* contains the name of the court reporter rather than the abbreviation "U.S." These reporters were Dallas (Dall.), Cranch (Cr.), Wheaton (Wheat.), Peters (Pet.), Howard (How.), Black (Bl.), and Wallace (Wall.). Thus, for example, the case of *McCulloch* v. *Maryland*, decided in 1819, is cited as 4 Wheat. 316.

separately published in the *Federal Supplement,* cited as "F. Supp." Decisions of the highest court of each state are collected in separate series referred to by the abbreviation of the specific state's name. The convention of citing the volume number before, and the page number after, the abbreviation of the series title is followed in references to these lower-court decisions. State supreme court decisions are also collected into a series of seven regional reports, each of which is published separately by the West Publishing Company. Those, with their abbreviations, are the Northeastern (N.E.), Atlantic (A.), Northwestern (N.W.), Southeastern (S.E.), Southern (So.), Southwestern (S.W.), and Pacific (P.), Reports.

METHODS OF REVIEW

Following the case title in the *United States Reports* is a succinct statement of the method whereby the case was brought to the Supreme Court from the court which last heard it. For example:

GRAY, CHAIRMAN OF THE GEORGIA STATE
DEMOCRATIC EXECUTIVE COMMITTEE
ET AL. *v.*. SANDERS.

APPEAL FROM THE UNITED STATES DISTRICT COURT
FOR THE NORTHERN DISTRICT OF GEORGIA.

GIDEON *v.* WAINWRIGHT, CORRECTIONS
DIRECTOR.

CERTIORARI TO THE SUPREME COURT OF FLORIDA.

Appeal and certiorari are the two most important methods for bringing cases to the attention of the Supreme Court. The litigant who lost in the court which last heard the case has the right to petition the Supreme Court to review the lower court's decision. Depending upon the issue which his case contains and how the lower courts decided that issue, the appellant will seek either a writ of appeal or a writ of certiorari from the Supreme Court.

Since 1925, the Court has had complete discretion over its dockets (the cases it accepts for decision). Hence, the distinction between appeal and certiorari no longer has operational significance.

For the most part, the losing party may petition the Court for a writ of appeal where a state supreme court has declared a federal action to be unconstitutional or a state action not to be unconstitutional; where a lower federal court has decided against the United States in a criminal proceeding; where the United States has brought action under the antitrust laws or Interstate Commerce Act; or in a federal district court suit to restrain the enforcement of a state or federal statute on the grounds of unconstitutionality.

The writ of certiorari, on the other hand, provides an avenue to the Court in those cases not covered by the writ of appeal. Thus, certiorari extends to any civil or criminal case in the federal courts of appeals regardless of the parties, the status of the case, or the amount in controversy. Certiorari jurisdiction also allows the Court to review state court decisions where the validity of a federal treaty or statute is questioned or where a state statute is found to be unconstitutional. Any state court decision which involves the construction and application of the federal Constitution, treaties, or laws, or the determination of a federal title, right, privilege, or immunity similarly falls within the compass of the Supreme Court's certiorari jurisdiction. Consequently, the scope of the Court's certiorari jurisdiction is much broader than that afforded by the writ of appeal. If four justices vote to grant certiorari, the Court will then hear and decide the case.[13]

---

[13]Cases may also be brought to the Court's attention by means of certification. This seldom used method involves a request by a federal court of appeals or the Court of Claims to answer certain questions so that the proper decision may be made in the case. This method differs from appeal and certiorari in that it is not within the control of the litigants; only a court of appeals or the Court of Claims itself may request review by this means. A recent example was *United States* v. *Barnett*, 376 U.S. 681 (1964), where the Supreme Court held that a former Mississippi governor could be punished for criminal contempt of court without a jury trial in proceedings before a federal court of appeals. The Court may also review cases brought to it by means of an extraordinary writ of mandamus or prohibition. These, however, are used even less frequently than certification. Cases decided prior to the New Deal often came to the Court by means of a writ of

CASE SUMMARY

Following the case title and the statement indicating how the case reached the Court is a summary of the case prepared by the editorial staff of the publisher of the series in which the case appears. Summaries in the *U.S. Reports* are prepared by the Court's reporter. These summaries, or headnotes as they are sometimes called, are an index of the legal points contained in the opinions of the case, but they are too brief to take the place of a full-scale study of the case itself. Furthermore, with their legal orientation, they frequently overlook or deemphasize points and issues of major political significance. Nor do the summaries in the *U.S. Reports* concern themselves with the dissenting or concurring opinions which are not only useful indicators of the attitudes of individual justices but also propose alternative ways of resolving the policy issues present in the case for decision.

AMICUS CURIAE PARTICIPANTS

The last of the introductory material contained in the printed court decisions is a list of the attorneys representing the litigants in the case. Because of the bearing which many Supreme Court cases have upon the public interest, the Court will occasionally allow a third party to be heard as *amicus curiae* ("friend of the court"). These organizations and their attorneys are also listed in this section of the introductory material of the case. The purpose of *amicus curiae* participation is to provide representation in the decision-making process of the Court to an interested and affected third party who is not a formal litigant in the case.[14] By allowing this, the Court hopes to expand its awareness of the implications its decision in the case may have upon public policy. Occasionally a third party participates as *amicus curiae* when the Court believes there is some weakness in the legal talent employed by the principal party to the dispute. The national gov-

---

error. This method, now abolished, allowed the Court far less discretion over the cases it would hear than it has had under certiorari.

[14]The best statement of the role of the "friend of the Court" with respect to the U.S. Supreme Court may be found in Samuel Krislov, "The Amicus Curiae Brief: From Friendship to Advocacy," *Yale Law Journal* 72 (1963), 694–721.

ernment, in the person of the Solicitor General or one of his aides, has most often functioned in this *amicus curiae* capacity because a private party, primarily concerned with winning his case, and perhaps unable to secure the most competent legal counsel, is frequently unconcerned with or ignorant of the implications which the Court's decision in his case may have upon the future course of American government and society.

A third party may participate as *amicus curiae* either at his own request or at that of the Court itself. Although the participation of the *amicus curiae* is most often limited to the presentation of a written brief containing arguments why the Court should uphold or reverse the decision of the lower court, occasionally the Court will allow an *amicus curiae* to participate in the oral argument before the Court as well.

Many, if not most, of the cases brought before the Court involve interest-group activity. The American Civil Liberties Union, the NAACP, business and labor organizations are frequently involved in Supreme Court litigation. Not only do they seek to appear in an *amicus curiae* capacity in cases affecting their interests, but in addition their attorneys often directly represent the litigants. Furthermore, interest groups regularly seek attainment of their objectives by resort to the courts. In their desire to change public policy, interest groups try to secure the "proper" case for judicial consideration, the one which presents their contention in the most favorable light.[15]

THE "FACTS"

In most Supreme Court decisions, the opinion of the Court begins with a recitation of the factual situation out of which the litigation arose; once in a while, though, additional facts may be found scattered throughout an opinion. Since the Supreme Court

---

[15]Excerpts from the major work dealing with the role of interest groups in the judicial process may be found in Glendon A. Schubert, *Constitutional Politics* (New York: Holt, Rinehart and Winston, 1960), pp. 69–82; Robert Scigliano, *The Courts* (Boston: Little, Brown and Co., 1962), pp. 176–199; and Walter F. Murphy and C. Herman Pritchett, *Courts, Judges, and Politics* (New York: Random House, 1961), chap. 8.

is an appellate tribunal, it must ascertain whether the law has been correctly applied to the "facts" of the case. The determination of the "facts" is primarily the responsibility of the trial court, the court which originally heard the dispute, but the Supreme Court's focus upon questions of law rather than facts does not mean that the latter are of no significance. The "facts" determine not only what law or constitutional provision is relevant to the resolution of the dispute, but whether the matter is of sufficient importance to warrant consideration by the Supreme Court. Although the "facts" may appear to be trivial, the rendering of a decision on the matter by the Supreme Court belies any apparent insignificance in the factual setting out of which the case arose.[16] Thus, for example, the factual circumstances in *Wickard* v. *Filburn*, 317 U.S. 111 (1942), provided the vehicle for one of the broadest definitions ever given Congress' regulatory powers. And yet nothing more was involved here than the commonplace situation of a farmer who grew a few acres of wheat on his farm which he intended to feed his livestock. On the other hand, the "facts" of a given case may be such that they hold the entire nation's attention. Such was the situation in the Pentagon Papers Case, 403 U.S. 713 (1971), which concerned newspaper publication of secret Vietnam War documents, and in *Oregon* v. *Mitchell*, 400 U.S. 112 (1970), which concerned the constitutionality of Congress' attempt to lower the voting age to eighteen. Even so, the significance of the Court's decision in *Oregon* v. *Mitchell* is likely to be of purely symbolic significance, given the tendency of young people to vote the least frequently of all age groups and their tendency to vote in the same partisan fashion as their parents.

The moral of *Wickard* v. *Filburn* and *Oregon* v. *Mitchell*, then, is that the "facts" in a given case are no necessary indicator of the importance of the Court's decision. But even though the "facts" do not provide a guide to the significance of the case, they are

---

[16]An exception may be the handful of cases per term dealing with the purely factual question of whether there is sufficient evidence to uphold the claim of an injured workman for compensation under federal law. The Supreme Court will also resolve decisional differences between two federal courts of appeals even though the issue is of minor moment.

nonetheless an integral part of the case along with the issues and the opinions themselves. Without knowledge of what the "facts" are, it is simply not possible to understand what a case is all about.

Inasmuch as the Supreme Court is primarily concerned with resolving the issues underlying a case rather than determining the "facts" of the case, the Court in its opinion merely provides a summary or digest of the "facts" as found by the trial court which previously heard the case. An example of a fairly typical statement of "facts" is that provided in the important case of *Gideon* v. *Wainwright*, 372 U.S. 335 (1963):

Petitioner was charged in a Florida state court with having broken and entered a poolroom with intent to commit a misdemeanor. This offense is a felony under Florida law. Appearing in court without funds and without a lawyer, petitioner asked the court to appoint counsel for him, whereupon the following colloquy took place:

"THE COURT: Mr. Gideon, I am sorry, but I cannot appoint Counsel to represent you in this case. Under the laws of the State of Florida, the only time the Court can appoint Counsel to represent a Defendant is when that person is charged with a capital offense. I am sorry, but I will have to deny your request to appoint Counsel to defend you in this case.

"THE DEFENDANT: The United States Supreme Court says I am entitled to be represented by Counsel."

Put to trial before a jury, Gideon conducted his defense about as well as could be expected from a layman. He made an opening statement to the jury, cross-examined the State's witnesses, presented witnesses in his own defense, declined to testify himself, and made a short argument "emphasizing his innocence to the charge contained in the Information filed in this case." The jury returned a verdict of guilty, and petitioner was sentenced to serve five years in the state prison. Later, petitioner filed in the Florida Supreme Court this habeas corpus petition attacking his conviction and sentence on the ground that the trial court's refusal to appoint counsel for him denied him rights "guaranteed by the Constitution and the Bill of Rights by the United States Government." Treating the petition for habeas corpus as properly before it, the State Supreme Court, "upon consideration thereof" but without an opinion, denied all relief. Since 1942, when *Betts* v. *Brady*, 316 U.S. 455, was decided by a divided Court, the problem of a defendant's federal constitutional right to counsel in a state court has been a continuing source of controversy and litigation in both state and federal courts. To give this problem another review here, we granted certiorari. 370 U.S. 908.

Since Gideon was proceeding *in forma pauperis*,[17] we appointed counsel to represent him and requested both sides to discuss in their briefs and oral arguments the following: "Should this Court's holding in *Betts* v. *Brady*, 316 U.S. 455, be reconsidered?"

More often the statement of "facts" is of considerably greater length, either because the case has seen much more lower court litigation or because the factual circumstances are much more complicated. An example of the former is *Griffin* v. *School Board of Prince Edward County*, 377 U.S. 218 (1964), which had been in litigation since 1951 and which was one of the cases originally decided by the Supreme Court in the famous School Segregation Cases of 1954. Exemplifying a complicated factual situation was *Reynolds* v. *Sims*, 377 U.S. 533 (1964), wherein the constitutionality of malapportioned state legislatures was decided. Here the "facts" involved a specification of the various provisions of the Alabama Constitution dealing with legislative apportionment as well as the specification of the population imbalance between various sections of the state as found by the lower court.

On occasion, a statement of "facts" is also found in a dissenting or concurring opinion. This kind of statement is inserted where the minority believes the majority has misstated or ignored relevant aspects of the case. In *Mapp* v. *Ohio*, 367 U.S. 643 (1961), as the majority treated the factual circumstances, the case became one involving an unreasonable search and seizure. Justice Harlan, dissenting, maintained that the "facts" were such that the case was concerned with the possession of obscene material. Where a justice views the "facts" differently from his colleagues, he will also usually perceive the issues presented in the case for decision to be other than those decided by the other justices.

---

[17]An *in forma pauperis* petition is one where a plaintiff is unable to bear the financial costs of appealing a case to a higher court. Conditions under which a person may bring legal action *in forma pauperis* are specified in state and federal statutes. A person allowed to proceed *in forma pauperis* does not pay the fees normally charged a person appealing the verdict of a lower court. The federal *in forma pauperis* statute is sufficiently broad to insure that no litigant is denied access to the Court because of financial hardship.

THE ISSUES

A statement of the issue or issues present in a case for decision is normally found either before or immediately after the recitation of the "facts" in the case. They are usually stated succinctly, as can be seen in the following examples:

Once again we are called upon to consider the scope of the provision of the First Amendment . . . which declares that "Congress shall make no law respecting an establishment of religion, or prohibiting the free exercise thereof. . . ." These . . . cases present the issues in the context of state action requiring that schools begin each day with readings from the Bible. (*Abington School District* v. *Schempp*, 374 U.S. 203 [1963])

This appeal involves a single question: the constitutionality of § 6 of the Subversive Activities Control Act of 1950, . . . (*Aptheker* v. *Secretary of State*, 378 U.S. 500 [1964])

The cases before us raise questions which go to the roots of our concepts of American criminal jurisprudence: the restraints society must observe consistent with the Federal Constitution in prosecuting individuals for crime. More specifically, we deal with the admissibility of statements obtained from an individual who is subjected to custodial police interrogation and the necessity for procedures which assure that the individual is accorded his privilege under the Fifth Amendment to the Constitution not to be compelled to incriminate himself. (*Miranda* v. *Arizona*, 384 U.S. 436 [1966]).

This is a civil suit charging a violation of § 7 of the Clayton Act, by reason of the acquisition of the stock and assets of Pacific Northwest Pipeline Corp. . . . by El Paso Natural Gas Co. . . .
The ultimate issue revolves around the question whether the acquisition substantially lessened competition in the sale of natural gas in California . . . (*United States* v. *El Paso Natural Gas Co.*, 376 U.S. 651 [1964])

These typical statements of the issues presented in Supreme Court cases exemplify the two kinds of issues which the Court's cases present: In the Schempp, Aptheker, and Miranda Cases, the Court was faced with a constitutional question. In *El Paso* the issue was one of statutory construction. Note that although the Aptheker Case involves an Act of Congress, the issue does not pertain to the interpretation or application of the Subversive Activities Control Act, but rather the question of whether Section 6 is compatible with the Constitution or not. If the issue in the Aptheker Case had been, for example, whether Aptheker was subject to the provisions of Section 6, whether Section 6 conflicted with some other law passed by Congress, or what certain terminology employed therein meant, then the issue would be one of statutory construction.

In the popular mind, the focus of Supreme Court decision making has been upon constitutional adjudication, cases where the Court has been called upon to apply the relevant provision of the Constitution to the matter at hand. Admittedly, the landmark decisions of American constitutional history are primarily composed of such cases. Even so, cases pertaining only to the construction and application of federal statutes (statutory construction) should not be ignored. In the area of national economic regulation, a case which turns on a constitutional question is now a rarity. And at the present time between one-third and two-fifths of the cases decided by the Court in an average term relate to economic and fiscal policy. Hence, such matters as business monopoly and mergers, trade practices and pricing policy, the regulation of the transportation and communications industries, the field of labor-management relations, and federal taxation are decided by the Court by construing the relevant provisions of Congressional statutes or the rules and regulations of the federal regulatory commissions, such as the Federal Trade Commission, the Interstate Commerce Commission, the National Labor Relations Board, the Federal Communications Commission, and the Securities and Exchange Commission. Outside the areas of economic and fiscal policy, a number of important cases dealing with immigration and naturalization, deportation, internal security, criminal procedure, selective service, and poverty law have also been decided on nonconstitutional grounds.

The issues contained in a case are initially stipulated in the request for a writ of certiorari or appeal. An attorney filing a petition for Supreme Court review of his case will typically base his request upon as many relevant issues as possible in the hope that at least four of the justices will find at least one of them sufficiently important to grant review. As part of the control which it has over its docket, the Court is free to define for itself the bases on which it accepts a case for review. Quite frequently the Court will avoid the constitutional issues presented and instead choose to decide the case on narrow technical grounds. Nor is it uncommon for the Court to decide a case on the basis of an issue which was not stipulated in the original request for a writ of certiorari or appeal. This careful selection of issues in a case, or the grounds for a decision, is one of the most important ways in which the Court makes (or doesn't make) policy. It is also used as a method for avoiding issues that are especially controversial.

This process is well illustrated by litigation pertaining to the death penalty. The broadest question related hereto is whether the cruel and unusual punishment provision of the Eighth Amendment prohibits a death sentence. To date, the Court has not addressed itself to this question. Also based upon the Eighth Amendment is the question of whether a death sentence for rape is prohibited. In 1963 Justices Goldberg, Douglas, and Brennan unsuccessfully urged the Court to decide this question where human life was "neither taken nor endangered" (*Rudolph* v. *Alabama*, 375 U.S. 889). In December 1970, however, a three-judge federal court of appeals unanimously held that the death penalty in such circumstances did constitute cruel and unusual punishment. (Interestingly, one of the participating judges was Clement Haynsworth, whose promotion to the Supreme Court had received Senatorial rejection one year earlier.) If this decision becomes a precedent, a third question will be minimized: Does the fact that blacks are sentenced to death for raping whites, but whites almost never for raping blacks, constitute race discrimination? The Court refused to consider this question when it granted review in the widely publicized case of *Maxwell* v. *Bishop*, 393 U.S. 997 (1968). The two questions the Court did agree to consider in this case were: Is due process violated by allowing a jury absolute discretion to impose the death penalty? And does the simultaneous determination of guilt and punishment by a jury violate the accused's privilege against self-incrimination? But when the Court announced its decision in the *Maxwell* case in 1970 (398 U.S. 262), it decided neither of these questions. Instead, by a 6–1 vote, it remanded the case back to the federal district court for consideration of Maxwell's claim that opponents of capital punishment were excluded from the jury that tried him. In *Witherspoon* v. *Illinois*, 391 U.S. 510 (1968), the Court had ruled such exculsion to violate due process of law, and had vacated a number of other death sentences prior to Maxwell on this basis. This is an example of how the Court can make policy (*i.e.*, forbidding the imposition of capital punishment) while at the same time avoiding a decision as to whether or not capital punishment is unconstitutional (a decision that might lead to considerable negative reaction). On the other hand, the two questions that the Court was to have decided in the grant of certiorari to Maxwell were not completely disregarded. These became, instead, the bases for granting certiorari in two cases on the same day that Maxwell was decided (*McGautha* v. *California* and *Crampton* v. *Ohio*, 398 U.S. 936). In its decision in *McGautha* and *Crampton*, 402 U.S. 183 (1971), the Court, by a 6–3 vote, held that due process was not violated by allowing a jury absolute discretion to impose a death penalty; nor does a jury's simultaneous determination of guilt and punishment constitute self-incrimination.

There the matter rests. The Court will undoubtedly rule whether the death sentence constitutes a cruel and unusual punishment in the near future. The probability is high that at least six justices will hold that it does not. Apart from executive clemency, the only recourse likely to be available to inmates of death row is the *Witherspoon* holding. This should be sufficient, however, since the overwhelming majority, if not all, death row inmates were probably tried by juries from which persons having scruples against capital punishment were automatically excluded.

The Court's frequent hesitancy in addressing novel constitutional issues, although frustrating to those whose lives and interests are at stake, is nonetheless politically significant. It illuminates the conflict between the Court, on the one hand, and Congress, the President, the states, or affected publics on the other. On the death penalty issue, for example, the Nixon Administration has communicated to the Court (through Solicitor General Griswold, arguing as *amicus curiae*) its opposition to any alteration in the states' death penalty procedures. Also not to be overlooked is the probability of division within the Court itself; different justices manifest conservative, moderate, and liberal policy preferences. In the *Maxwell* case, for example, a vote on one of the other constitutional issues involved may have produced a result quite different than 6–1.

In their perception of the issues contained in the cases that they decide, the justices by no means treat each case as though it raises a unique issue or issues.[18] This is not to deny that each case is unique from the standpoint of complete detail. The evidence, however, strongly suggests that the vast majority of cases are treated by the justices as though they raise an issue, or issues, common to some, but not to all, other cases. As is explained in the section concerning the personal factor in Supreme Court decision making, each justice has a distinctive combination of positions on the dimensions of voting behavior. Moreover, each justice will distinctively perceive the issue(s) contained in a given case as more or less extreme. Thus, for example, if only one of the justices finds merit in a person's claim that his civil rights or liberties have been abridged, the probability is high that that single justice will be Douglas. But this does not mean that the justices have largely unique perceptions of the issues. As we shall see, the fact that more than 80% of the Court's decisions may be explained and the votes of the individual justices predicted on the basis of their response to but three "values" indicates agreement on the definition of issues.

THE OPINIONS

The overwhelming bulk of a Supreme Court case is composed of the opinions. The "facts" as well as the issues to be decided are found in the opinions, as is the decision or judgment which the Court makes in each case it hears. Opinions are of three kinds: the opinion of the Court, dissenting opinions, and concurring opinions.

The opinion of the Court is the one in which a majority of the participating justices join. It is either written by an individual justice, whose name appears at the head of the opinion, or is a

---

[18]See Harold J. Spaeth and David J. Peterson, "The Analysis and Interpretation of Dimensionality: The Case of Civil Liberties Decision Making," *Midwest Journal of Political Science* 15 (1971), 415.

collective enterprise in which no single name appears as author. An opinion of the latter sort is labeled *"per curiam"* to indicate that it is a collective production. Generally, the *per curiam* opinion is considerably shorter than the individual justice's opinion and is concerned with less difficult and significant questions.

The importance of the opinion of the Court is that it is the vehicle whereby the Court performs its policy-making function. Whereas the decision or judgment of the Court simply stipulates who wins and who loses, and how the case is disposed of (as explained in the last section of this book), the opinion of the Court presents the constitutional and legal principles on which the majority bases its decision. The principles governing the decision are binding upon the lower courts in all similar cases subsequently decided, and they serve, as well, as precedents to guide the course of future Supreme Court decision making.

For an opinion to be considered the opinion of the Court, whether it be individually written or *per curiam*, a majority of the participating justices must agree with its contents. Occasionally, perhaps in as many as a half-dozen cases a term, the justices may not be able to agree on an opinion of the Court. Such a situation results where a majority agrees on the disposition of the case but not on an opinion supporting this judgment. The indication that a case contains no opinion of the Court is usually phrased as in the first of the three 1966 Censorship Cases, *Memoirs* v. *Massachusetts*, 383 U.S. 413, which decided whether or not the book, *Fanny Hill*, was obscene:

MR. JUSTICE BRENNAN announced the judgment of the Court and delivered an opinion in which THE CHIEF JUSTICE and MR. JUSTICE FORTAS join.

The absence of an opinion of the Court need not lessen the impact of the decision, however, depending upon how unqualifiedly the concurring justices associate themselves with the judgment of the Court. In the above case, three additional justices concurred in the judgment of the Court, with the result that by a 6–3 vote *Fanny Hill* was declared not to be obscene.

Justices who do not agree with the opinion and judgment of the Court are free to dissent or concur. A dissenting or concurring justice is not required to write an opinion in support of his vote. But it has been somewhat unusual in recent terms for a justice to disagree with the majority without providing a statement of the reasons for his disagreement.

A dissenting opinion is simply one where a justice disagrees with the majority's decision in the case. Dissenting opinions occur much more frequently than concurring opinions. The latter signify a justice's agreement with the Court's decision, but disagreement with the reasoning of the opinion of the Court whereby the decision was reached. Occasionally, too, a justice may concur in the opinion as well as the decision of the Court but nonetheless feel obliged to add a few of his own comments. Thus, for example, Justice Stewart concurred in both the opinion and judgment of the Court in the first two of the great apportionment decisions, *Baker* v. *Carr*, 369 U.S. 186 (1962), and *Gray* v. *Sanders*, 372 U.S. 368 (1963). He did so because he felt compelled to restate the issue before the Court for decision. In his view the other minority opinions clouded the issue, and he wished to emphasize that he agreed only with what the Court had decided and no more.

Data compiled by the clerk of the Supreme Court for the two most recent terms for which they are available[19] portray the relative frequency of dissenting and concurring opinions:

Table 1. Frequency of Dissenting and Concurring Opinions

Term	Opinions		
	of the Court	Dissenting	Concurring
1968	99	77	48
1969	88	73	49

If the dissenting and concurring opinions are added together, an average of 1.3 minority opinions were filed in each case decided by an opinion of the Court. My figures show that each dissenting opinion on the average represented 1.8 votes, with each concur-

---

[19]The 1968 and 1969 terms. The former was the last term of the Warren Court, while 1969 was the first term of the Burger Court. The data are published in *Congressional Quarterly*, August 7, 1970, p. 2017.

ring opinion representing an average of 1.4 votes. In other words, most of the time at least one other justice joins with the author of the dissenting opinion, whereas a justice writing a concurring opinion more often than not concurs alone.

Politically, certain by-products result from dissenting and concurring opinions, especially the former. Their presence constitutes a public debate from the Bench over public policies under consideration. And since a single decision rarely settles a policy even when the Court is unanimous, dissenting opinions may spur supporters of the defeated policy to continue the struggle. In addition, a dissenting opinion suggests a line of attack for attorneys and others representing the defeated interest to follow in subsequent attempts to change the law.

6

Coalition Formation and Opinion Assignment

One of the rules governing the decision making of the Supreme Court is that the senior justice in length of service on the Court who votes with the majority has the power to assign the opinion of the Court. By reason of his position, the chief justice is defined as the most senior justice. Thus, over the period of the Warren Court (1953–1969), the justices who had primary responsibility for assigning opinions were Warren himself, plus the two justices longest on the Court—Black and Frankfurter.

The discussion of the personal factor in Supreme Court decision making in chapter 9 advances the argument—with supporting evidence—that the justices are goal-oriented—that they are motivated to vote as they do on the basis of their personal policy preferences. On the basis that the justices are goal-oriented, then the means of translating one's goal orientation into authoritative policy becomes important. The means available is the formation of a coalition that creates the majority opinion.

The Court's decision making, of course, is determined by the votes of the justices. But decision making is limited to the determination of who wins and who loses a given case, and whether the decision of the lower court is affirmed or reversed. As explained in the first chapter of this book, it is the Court's policy-making function that has enabled it to shape and direct the course of American government and society. The vehicle whereby the Court performs this policy-making function is its opinion. Contained herein are the broad constitutional and legal principles that govern the decision in the case at hand, that bind the lower courts in all similar cases, and that serve as precedents for the Court's future decisions.

Recent analysis[20] has shown that the formation of the winning coalition is governed by William Riker's size principle.[21] Riker's theory assumes, in relevant part, that (1) a decision must be made by a predetermined number of people; (2) each decision maker must either win or lose; (3) the winning decision makers determine who will share the benefits of winning; (4) the division of the payoff among the winners may be disproportionate; and (5) a member of the winning side may withdraw before the decision is made if he so chooses. If these five conditions are met, the size principle holds and a minimum winning coalition will be formed.

The five conditions are met in Supreme Court decision making: (1) There are nine justices. (2) Each participating justice either joins the opinion of the Court or he dissents or concurs. (3) Once a majority opinion coalition is formed (requiring five justices if eight or nine members participate, which almost always occurs), the coalition members need not consider the policy preferences of an additional justice in their opinion. The additional justice(s) may also join the opinion of the Court, but not at the price of having the opinion altered to accommodate his views. (4) In order to secure a fifth justice, a coalition may disproportionately cater to his policy preferences. (5) If, in order to attract an additional member to the coalition, concessions are made that one of the original justices disapproves of, he may dissociate himself from the majority by dissenting or concurring.

Application of the size principle to opinion coalitions in the Supreme Court requires that two distinctive situations be recognized:[22] issue areas which do not pose a threat to the Court's power and authority, and those that do. Examples of the latter are matters upon which Congress is threatening to alter the

---

[20]David W. Rohde, "A Theory of the Formation of Opinion Coalitions in the U.S. Supreme Court," in Richard G. Niemi and Herbert F. Weisberg (eds.), *Probability Models of Collective Decision Making* (Columbus: Merrill, 1971).

[21]Willima H. Riker, *The Theory of Political Coalitions* (New Haven: Yale University Press, 1962), chap. 2.

[22]Rohde, *op. cit.* fn. 20 *supra*.

Court's jurisdiction—e.g., internal security in the 1950s and criminal procedure in the 1960s; alteration in the size of the Court—e.g., the Court packing proposal of 1937; or issues where the probability of public compliance is low—e.g., school desegregation.

In issue areas posing no threat to the Court's institutional integrity, the size principle should operate, with the result that the frequency of five-member coalitions should statistically significantly exceed the frequency expected on a random basis. Conversely, the size principle should not operate to a statistically significant degree in issue areas posing an environmental threat to the Court. The rationale here is that one or more of the justices will subordinate personal policy preferences for the sake of protecting the Court.

In an analysis of seventy-six cases decided in the 1953 through 1967 terms, in which the Court stated that a First Amendment issue was raised, the fifty-eight cases in five non-threat issue areas resulted in thirty-seven minimum winning coalitions. The eighteen cases in the three threat issue areas produced only five minimum winning coalitions. Both results were statistically significant.[23]

Given the operation of the size principle in most of the Court's decisions, who within the minimum winning coalition will be assigned the opinion of the Court? As will be shown in the section pertaining to the personal factor in Supreme Court decision making, the justices are motivated to vote the way they do by their personal policy preferences. Because the expression of these preferences is accomplished most authoritatively through the opinion of the Court, the ideal solution is for the assigner of the majority opinion to assign the opinion to himself. This is not always possible because one of the internal rules of the Court is that the opinion writing workload should be spread equally among all the members of the Court. Hence, over the course of a term, the ideal situation from the standpoint of this rule is that each of the justices should have written the same number of

---

[23]Ibid. In order to avoid a tautological argument, the threat and non-threat issue areas were operationally defined and independently measured.

majority opinions. But because of the variance in the justices' value goals, some justices will be in majority coalitions much more frequently than others. Consequently, this rule is only approximated.

Also governing the assignment of opinions is the fact that the assignee will be forced to bargain and make policy concessions in order to create a majority coalition. Such compromise is essential because a majority of the participating justices is necessary to an opinion of the Court.

Therefore, the most rational course for the opinion assigner, within the constraints of the foregoing rules, is to assign the opinion to the justice whose position is closest to his own on the issue in question. This hypothesis was tested on a set of 480 civil liberties cases decided by the Warren Court.[24] These cases were divided into thirty-four cumulative scales,[25] each of which constituted a separate issue area. The position "closest" to the opinion assigner was defined as the assigner himself plus the justice ranking closest to him on the various cumulative scales. The results show that all three of the major opinion assigners—Warren and the two senior associate justices, Black and Frankfurter—behaved compatibly with the above hypothesis.

Although the opinion assigner and the justice closest to him are advantaged in writing opinions, the importance of the fifth justice in the formation of a winning coalition indicates that he also should receive more than his share of opinion assignments. The data show this to be the case, with the justices occupying the other positions being assigned less than their proportionate share of opinions.[26]

Clearly, then, personal policy preferences dominate coalition formation and opinion assignment. The size principle dictates five-member coalitions a disproportionate amount of the time. In order to ensure congruence between his own personal policy

---

[24]David W. Rohde, "Policy Goals, Strategic Choice and Majority Opinion Assignments in the U.S. Supreme Court." Paper presented at the Conference on Theories of Collective Behavior, University of Pennsylvania, Dec. 10–11, 1970.

[25]See the chapter entitled, "The Personal Factor in Supreme Court Decision Making," pp. 64–65, for a description of cumulative scales.

[26]Rohde, *op. cit.* fn. 24 *supra*.

preferences and the opinion of the Court, opinion assigners write the opinion themselves, assign it to the justice whose views are closest to his own, or assign it to the pivotal fifth member of the decisional coalition. Such behavior is not invariably manifested, however. Threat situations will cause some justices to subordinate policy goals to the Court's institutional integrity, and the rule that each justice should write one-ninth of the opinions of the Court precludes exclusive assignment of opinions on the basis of policy goals.

7

The Problem of Clarity in Supreme Court Opinions

A major problem with regard to the opinions of the Court is that they are occasionally not as clear or as certain as to their meaning as they might be. Such unclarity creates a problem not only for the lower courts that are charged with implementing the Court's decisions but also for Congress, executive officials, and even the public at large. One may argue, of course, that the Court decides only the specific case before it, and that its decision applies only to the litigants in that case. This argument is true so far as it goes, but it overlooks the leadership which the Court is expected to provide the lower federal courts and the state judicial systems. It is a fact of American life that the Court's decisions have an impact which goes far beyond the narrow interests of the parties directly affected by the litigation before the Court. Indeed, the Court consciously limits its decision making to cases presenting important public policy issues. As a result, cases brought to the Court's attention often take the form of a "class action." This is a suit brought by specific individuals on behalf of themselves and all other persons similarly situated. Consequently, when the opinion of the Court is somewhat obscure the task of lower courts involved in related litigation becomes more difficult.

A good example of lack of clarity is *Jencks* v. *United States*, 353 U.S. 657 (1957). This case dealt with a perennial criminal law problem, that of the right of a defendant to secure material discrediting the testimony of prosecution witnesses. Jencks, a labor-union official, was charged with falsely swearing that he was not affiliated with the Communist Party in an affidavit filed with the

National Labor Relations Board. The Court held that he was entitled to inspect the reports of two F.B.I. informers as to the events and activities to which they had testified at his trial. With respect to Jencks, the Court's decision was clear enough. But Congress, the F.B.I., and various federal administrative agencies felt that the decision posed a threat to effective law enforcement, particularly in the area of internal security. Their fears were strongly phrased in Justice Clark's biting dissent:

> Unless the Congress changes the rule announced by the Court today, those intelligence agencies of our Government engaged in law enforcement may as well close up shop, for the Court has opened their files to the criminal and thus afforded him a Roman holiday for rummaging through confidential information as well as vital national secrets.

By overstating the majority's holding, a dissenting opinion may very well diminish if not destroy the essential clarity of the majority decision. It may be argued that this is what happened in the Jencks Case, that Clark's dissent heightened the fears and distrust of certain members of Congress toward the decision making of the Supreme Court in cases connected with questions of national security. Two weeks after the Jencks decision the Court handed down important decisions in *Watkins* v. *United States*, 354 U.S. 178, *Yates* v. *United States*, 354 U.S. 298, and *Sweezy* v. *New Hampshire*, 354 U.S. 234, in all of which the Court refused to support the position of the security minded, thus adding further fuel to the fire.[27]

Although Clark's dissent in the Jencks Case did not assert that the opinion of the Court was unclear, his tactic of overstating the majority's holding had essentially the same effect as if he had: it undermined the majority's position. Where a minority viewpoint asserting vagueness in the opinion of the Court seeks to alert the lower federal courts and the state judicial systems, Clark's tactic of overstating the majority's position was aimed instead at precipitating Congressional and public opposition to the deci-

---

[27]For the full story of the conflict between Congress and the Court over the issue of internal security, see Walter F. Murphy, *Congress and the Court* (Chicago: University of Chicago Press, 1962), pp. 127–268; and C. Herman Pritchett, *Congress Versus the Supreme Court, 1957–1960* (Minneapolis: University of Minnesota Press, 1961).

sion. As it happened, Congress enacted a law three months later which sought to confine the boundary lines of the Jencks decision. And although this law seems not to have insured complete clarity, presumably it did narrow the scope of subsequent Supreme Court decision making on this issue.[28]

Thus, lack of clarity in Supreme Court opinions takes two forms: (1) An opinion which the lower courts, federal or state, have difficulty in construing and applying. (2) An opinion whose implications create concern in the minds of Congress, executive officials, or the public at large. Needless to say, the problem of lack of clarity in a given decision need not be pointed out by a dissenting opinion for it to exist. But where a minority opinion does note the problem, the matter may receive more immediate and widespread attention than might otherwise be the case.

Undoubtedly an area of Supreme Court decision making where clarity is greatly obscured is obscenity. In *Roth* v. *United States* and *Alberts* v. *California*, 354 U.S. 476 (1957), the Court stated that obscene materials were not within the area of constitutionally protected speech and press. It then formulated the following test: "whether to the average person, applying contemporary community standards, the dominant theme of the material taken as a whole appeals to prurient interest." In *Manual Enterprises* v. *Day*, 370 U.S. 478 (1962), the Court ruled that for material to be obscene it must possess "patent offensiveness," and in 1964, in *Jacobellis* v. *Ohio*, 378 U.S. 184, it held that nothing could be proscribed "unless it is utterly without redeeming social importance." These three tests were held to be separate in the Censorship Cases of 1966 (383 U.S. 413, 463, and 502) and a fourth test was added: does the advertising and promotion demonstrate an intent to "pander?" Did the "leer of the sensualist" permeate the advertising? Has the publisher "deliberately emphasized the sexually provocative aspects of the work, in order to catch the salaciously disposed?" Then, in 1968, the Court held in *Ginsberg*

---

[28]See the subsequent Supreme Court decisions arising under the Jencks Act: *Palermo* v. *United States*, 360 U.S. 343 (1959); *Rosenberg* v. *United States*, 360 U.S. 367 (1959); *Campbell* v. *United States*, 365 U.S. 85 (1961); *Clancy* v. *United States*, 365 U.S. 312 (1961); *Campbell* v. *United States*, 373 U.S. 487 (1963); and *Evola* v. *United States*, 375 U.S. 32 (1963).

v. *New York*, 390 U.S. 629, that states may restrict the sorts of sex material that minors may read or see. Finally, the Court ruled in *Stanley* v. *Georgia*, 394 U.S. 557 (1969), that obscenity in the home is a constitutional right; that the power to regulate obscenity "does not extend to mere possession by the individual in the privacy of his own home."

In a radio and television interview shortly after his retirement, Chief Justice Warren said that obscenity was the Court's "most difficult area." It is, he said, "very difficult to write a verbal definition of what obscenity is."[29] Further evidence of this can be found in the fact that although ten of the fourteen obscenity cases formally decided after *Roth* and *Alberts* went against the government, a total of twenty-seven concurring opinions were filed in these fourteen cases. If dissenting opinions are included, the total rises to forty-six. Among the individual justices, Douglas and Black take the clearest position: government has no power to regulate any type of expression, obscene or not. The least clear position is that of Stewart: regulation of obscenity is "constitutionally limited to hard-core pornography. I shall not . . . attempt . . . to define the kinds of material I understand to be embraced within that shorthand description; and perhaps I could never succeed in intelligibly doing so. But I know it when I see it . . ."[30]

[29] *The New York Times*, June 27, 1969, p. 17.
[30] *Jacobellis* v. *Ohio*, 378 U.S. 184 (1964), at 197.

8

Theories of Judicial Interpretation

In its opinions, the Court must present arguments which support its decisions. The arguments which the justices use to substantiate their judgments will vary depending upon whether the issue is one of constitutional interpretation or statutory construction. It should be noted that the arguments which the justices employ can be used by those in the majority as well as by those who dissent or concur.

CONSTITUTIONAL INTERPRETATION

Analysis of the arguments employed in cases involving constitutional interpretation reveals that decisions in these cases are usually based upon one or more of the four following grounds.

1. The Intention of the Framers of the Constitution

An opinion based on this argument seeks to equate the decision of the Court with the objective which the Framers had in mind when they wrote the pertinent portion of the Constitution. Justices, as well as others employing this basis of argumentation, tend to restrict their concept of the Framers to that segment of the fifty-five delegates attending the Constitutional Convention who participated most frequently in the proceedings. Excluded from consideration as to intention are the delegates to the various state conventions who voted to ratify the Constitution. Also excluded are the people who selected the delegates who were to vote on the ratification of the Constitution.

When evaluating the adequacy of interpreting the Constitution on the basis of the Framers' intentions, it is pertinent to observe that knowledge of what happened in the Constitutional

Convention is almost entirely limited to the incomplete notes taken by James Madison. Moreover, many of the decisions made by the delegates were a result of compromise, and not infrequently the language employed to bridge differences of opinion was deliberately left vague and undefined. On the very basic question of the relationship of the national government to the states, for example, advocates of both centralization and decentralization argue that the Framers' intention is in exclusive support of their position.

2. The Meaning of the Words

This approach to constitutional interpretation is closely akin to that of the Framers' intentions in that each approach involves an attempt to justify decisions in terms of ostensible continuity with the past. The "meaning" approach is an attempt to define the words of the Constitution according to the meaning they had when the document was written. It consequently differs from recourse to the intent of the Framers in placing the highest premium upon lexicographic skill, whereas determination of the Framers' intent relies upon a broader use of historical data.

It is often said that an approach based upon the meaning of the words used in the Constitution, like that based on the intention of the Framers, makes American government the prisoner of its past, but it need not necessarily do so. To illustrate: Justice Black's opinion of the Court in *Wesberry* v. *Sanders*, 376 U.S. 1 (1964), held that the one man, one vote principle in the size of congressional districts was dictated by the provision of Article I of the Constitution which states that "the House of Representatives shall be composed of members chosen every second year by the people of the several states." By this one stroke, the historic rural domination of Congress was broken.

As a further example, access to the federal courts, under Article III of the Constitution, extends to "citizens of different states." On the basis of the eighteenth-century meaning of the words, corporations would not be allowed to bring suits in federal courts on the basis of diversity of state citizenship (residence) since, at the time of the adoption of the Constitution, corporations were clearly not considered "citizens." An approach based

upon the original meaning of the words in interpreting or applying this phrase of Article III would have a radical effect indeed
upon American business and the economic system, for denial of
access to the federal courts would effectively preclude corporate
enterprises from securing redress of their grievances through
legal means. Hence, neither the approach via the intention of the
Framers nor that via the meaning of the words necessarily makes
American society the prisoner of its past.

3. Logical Analysis

This approach is based upon the syllogism, which consists
quite simply of a major premise, a minor premise, and a conclusion. The major premise sets forth a proposition: for example, "a
law repugnant to the Constitution is void." The minor premise
states a fact related to the major premise: "law X is repugnant to
the Constitution." From the major and minor premises a conclusion automatically follows: "law X is unconstitutional." Quite
clearly the logical analysis approach depends upon the truth of
the premises which, in most litigation, is anything but self-evi-
dent. Hence, this approach should be mightily dependent upon
empirically substantiated facts. All too often, it is not.

Probably the classic example of the use of logical analysis in
American constitutional history is Chief Justice Marshall's opinion in *Marbury* v. *Madison*, 1 Cranch 137 (1803), which enunciated
the doctrine of judicial review, and thereby formally established
the court's policy-making function. It is pertinent to quote the
relevant passages in full:

> The question, whether an act, repugnant to the constitution, can
> become the law of the land, is a question deeply interesting to the United
> States; but, happily, not of an intricacy proportioned to its interest. It
> seems only necessary to recognise certain principles, supposed to have
> been long and well established, to decide it. . . .
> This original and supreme will organizes the government, and assigns
> to different departments their respective powers. It may either stop
> here, or establish certain limits not to be transcended by those depart-
> ments. The government of the United States is of the latter description.
> The powers of the legislature are defined and limited; and that those
> limits may not be mistaken or forgotten, the constitution is written. To
> what purpose are powers limited, and to what purpose is that limitation

committed to writing, if these limits may, at any time, be passed by those intended to be restrained? The distinction between a government with limited and unlimited powers is abolished, if those limits do not confine the persons on whom they are imposed, and if acts prohibited and acts allowed, are of equal obligation. It is a proposition too plain to be contested, that the constitution controls any legislative act repugnant to it; or that the legislature may alter the constitution by an ordinary act.

Between these alternatives, there is no middle ground. The constitution is either a superior paramount law, unchangeable by ordinary means, or it is on a level with ordinary legislative acts, and, like other acts, is alterable when the legislature shall please to alter it. If the former part of the alternative be true, then a legislative act, contrary to the constitution, is not law: if the latter part be true, then written constitutions are absurd attempts, on the part of the people, to limit a power, in its own nature, illimitable.

Certainly, all those who have framed written constitutions contemplate them as forming the fundamental and paramount law of the nation, and consequently, the theory of every such government must be, that an act of the legislature, repugnant to the constitution, is void. This theory is essentially attached to a written constitution, and is, consequently, to be considered, by this court, as one of the fundamental principles of our society. It is not, therefore, to be lost sight of, in the further consideration of this subject.

If an act of the legislature, repugnant to the constitution, is void, does it, notwithstanding its invalidity, bind the courts, and oblige them to give it effect? Or, in other words, though it be not law, does it constitute a rule as operative as if it was a law? This would be to overthrow, in fact, what was established in theory; and would seem, at first view, an absurdity too gross to be insisted on. It shall, however, receive a more attentive consideration.

It is, emphatically, the province and duty of the judicial department, to say what the law is. Those who apply the rule to particular cases, must of necessity expound and interpret that rule. If two laws conflict with each other, the courts must decide on the operation of each. So, if a law be in opposition to the constitution; if both the law and the constitution apply to a particular case, so that the court must either decide that case, conformable to the law, disregarding the constitution; or conformable to the constitution, disregarding the law; the court must determine which of these conflicting rules governs the case: this is of the very essence of judicial duty. If then, the courts are to regard the constitution, and the constitution is superior to any ordinary act of the legislature, the constitution, and not such ordinary act, must govern the case to which they both apply.

Those, then, who controvert the principle, that the constitution is to be considered, in court, as a paramount law, are reduced to the necessity of maintaining that courts must close their eyes on the constitution, and see only the law. This doctrine would subvert the very foundation of all written constitutions. It would declare that an act which, according to the principles and theory of our government, is entirely void, is yet, in practice, completely obligatory. It would declare, that if the legislature shall do what is expressly forbidden, such act, notwithstanding the express prohibition, is in reality effectual. It would be giving to the legislature a practical and real omnipotence, with the same breath which professes to restrict their powers within narrow limits. It is prescribing limits, and declaring that those limits may be passed at pleasure. . . .

Although the logic of this opinion may seem unassailable, it is just as logical to argue that since the President and Congress also take an oath to support the Constitution, they are at least as competent as the Supreme Court to determine whether an action of government conflicts with the Constitution. Hence, it follows that the President should not enforce a decision of the Court which in his view conflicts with the Constitution, nor the Congress defer to the Court's judgment that one of its laws is unconstitutional.

The basic weakness of logical analysis, then, is that it may be used independently of factual analysis and informed opinion and judgment. Justice Holmes stated the matter well:

The life of the law has not been logic: it has been experience. The felt necessities of the time, the prevalent moral and political theories, intuitions of public policy, avowed or unconscious, even the prejudices which judges share with their fellow-men, have had a good deal more to do than the syllogism in determining the rules by which men should be governed.[31]

Note also that although an argument based upon logical analysis is often termed "logical reasoning," it need not necessarily be reasonable. There is no necessary correlation between good logic and a reasonable decision. The premises of a syllogism may be unjust or even absurd, but so long as they are orderly and conform to the requirements of proper inference, they may not be inpugned as illogical.

The improper use of logic is most often seen in Supreme Court

---

[31]Quoted in Max Lerner (ed.), *The Mind and Faith of Justice Holmes* (New York: The Modern Library, 1943), pp. 51–52.

opinions where either a majority or minority opinion pushes an opposing argument to its logical conclusion. This tactic, known as the *argumentum ad horrendum*, is exemplified in Justice McReynolds' dissenting opinion in *Steward Machine Co. v. Davis*, 301 U.S. 548 (1937), in which the majority upheld the constitutionality of the Social Security Act. McReynolds "set out pertinent portions" of a veto message sent by President Franklin Pierce to the Senate May 3, 1854, to justify his opposition to the court's decision:

"It can not be questioned that if Congress has power to make provision for the indigent insane . . . it has the same power to provide for the indigent who are not insane, and thus to transfer to the Federal Government the charge of all the poor in all the States. It has the same power to provide hospitals and other local establishments for the care and cure of every species of human infirmity, and thus to assume all that duty of either public philanthropy or public necessity to the dependent, the orphan, the sick, or the needy which is now discharged by the States themselves or by corporate institutions or private endowments existing under the legislation of the States. The whole field of public beneficence is thrown open to the care and culture of the Federal Government. . . . If Congress may and ought to provide for any one of these objects, it may and ought to provide for them all. And if it be done in this case, what answer shall be given when Congress shall be called upon, as it doubtless will be, to pursue a similar course of legislation in the others? . . . The decision upon the principle in any one case determines it for the whole class. The question presented, therefore, clearly is upon the constitutionality and propriety of the Federal Government assuming to enter into a novel and vast field of legislation, namely, that of providing for the care and support of all those among the people of the United States who by any form of calamity become fit objects of public philanthropy. . . ."

4. The Adaptive Approach

Opinions based on this approach plead the necessity to accommodate the Constitution to changing times and circumstances. They consequently place a low value upon the intentions of the Framers, the original meaning of the words, or logical analysis. In general, an adaptive argument has been the mark of the liberal as opposed to the conservative justice. This statement should not be taken to mean that a liberal justice rarely, if ever, resorts to the other three approaches, or that the other three approaches are necessarily marked by fixity or rigidity.

The adaptive approach was well expressed by Chief Justice Marshall in *McCulloch* v. *Maryland*, 4 Wheaton 316 (1819), when he said "we must never forget that it is a constitution we are expounding," a constitution which is "intended to endure for ages to come, and consequently, to be *adapted* to the various crises of human affairs." [Italics added.] A lengthier statement is provided in Justice Holmes' dissent in *Lochner* v. *New York*, 198 U.S. 45 (1908):

> . . . a constitution is not intended to embody a particular economic theory, whether of paternalism and the organic relation of the citizen to the State or of *laissez faire*. It is made for people of fundamentally differing views, and the accident of our finding certain opinions natural and familiar or novel and even shocking ought not to conclude our judgment upon the question whether statutes embodying them conflict with the Constitution of the United States.
>
> General propositions do not decide concrete cases. The decision will depend on a judgment or intuition more subtle than any articulate major premise. . . . I think that the word liberty in the Fourteenth Amendment is perverted when it is held to prevent the natural outcome of a dominant opinion, unless it can be said that a rational and fair man necessarily would admit that the statute proposed would infringe fundamental principles as they have been understood by the traditions of our people and our law.

It is not correct to consider that adaptive arguments provide an open-ended range of choice. The justices are certainly not compelled by this approach to grant to a litigant everything he may want, nor are they allowed to legitimate whatever they may desire. At the heart of the adaptive approach is the recognition that though the Framers built exceedingly well, they were not capable of foreseeing the needs of a dynamic society this far into the future. The framework, then, is limiting; but within its confines change and alteration are permissible.

If an analysis of all the majority opinions written by members of the Supreme Court were made, it is certain that instances of the adaptive approach would be significantly less numerous than the other three. It appears in actual practice that justices have recourse to adaptive arguments only when, for one reason or another, they are precluded from using any of the other three approaches. In the popular mind, the Constitution has prescribed a fixed system of government. An argument based upon the need for change in accordance with changing circumstances and conditions may provoke opposition by those supportive of the status quo and those who require political certainty and governmental absolutes. Thus, as was noted, since the other approaches preserve the outward appearance of certainty and stability while allowing for substantive change, it would be foolhardy to risk antagonizing those who would accept the Court's judgment if the accompanying opinion were couched in terms of the intentions of the Framers, the original meaning of the words, or logical analysis. It is noteworthy that the precedent-breaking decisions the latter years of the Warren Court have been supported by arguments based on approaches other than the adaptive. Thus, for example, in the series of reapportionment cases, as well as those dealing with criminal procedure, obscenity, the establishment of religion, and the regulation of business and labor all the opinions of the Court avoided the adaptive approach.

All four theories of judicial interpretation discussed thus far apply to constitutional interpretation. Their presence in an opinion is evidence that the case contains constitutional issues. Nor are they mutually exclusive. The intentions of the Framers, the original meaning of the words, and logical analysis are often found blended together in a single opinion.

STATUTORY CONSTRUCTION

Supreme Court cases which do not contain constitutional issues concern questions of statutory construction. These include not only the interpretation and application of Acts of Congress, but the rules and regulations of the various federal regulatory agencies, the actions of the various units and officials of the executive branch of the national government, and the procedural rules and regulations prescribed by the Supreme Court to govern the operation of the federal judicial system.

There are two approaches which the Court uses in cases involving statutory construction: the argument via "plain meaning" and the argument via legislative history. The former is the equivalent of the approach via the meaning of the words in constitutional adjudication. The focus in the plain-meaning approach is upon the literal text of the statute and the objective is simply to construe what the statute says. By contrast, the legislative-history approach looks behind the face of the statute and seeks to ascertain the spirit of the law, to determine what the legislators really meant, as distinct from what the law says. Thus, this approach focuses upon legislative history; that is to say, upon the debates which attended the passage of the legislation, the majority and minority committee reports, the statements and views of the sponsors of the legislation, the testimony and comments of legislators, government officials, and interested private persons given at hearings when the legislation was proposed, and previous court decisions interpreting the statute. Among recent members of the Court, Justice Frankfurter was most closely associated with this approach.

Both these bases of argumentation have their weaknesses. Much legislation is a result of compromise, as a result of which terms are left undefined and provisions purposely vague.[32] Indeed, one may argue that vagueness and lack of definition are characteristic of virtually all major Congressional legislation. Obviously, then, the plain-meaning approach is something less than adequate. But though the plain meaning of statutory provisions is rarely apparent, the legislative-history approach does not necessarily provide a sure guide to Congressional intent. Many legislative committee reports are notably biased and self-serving; much of the content of the *Congressional Record* was never uttered on the floor of either the Senate or the House, and much that was spoken sheds little light on legislative intent. Consequently, the legislative-history approach is also somewhat less than adequate. One authority has derogated the legislative-history approach as "the psychoanalysis of Congress":

The assumption that congressmen behave like judges are supposed to behave just isn't supported by the available research findings, notwithstanding the fact that the highest title that one can bestow upon a member of the national legislature is to call him—even if he was only

---

[32]See Arthur S. Miller, "Statutory Language and the Purposive Use of Ambiguity," *Virginia Law Review* 42 (1956), 23–39.

a justice of the peace once forty years earlier—not "Senator," but "Judge." Such admiration is reciprocated by the majority of Supreme Court justices who have had no congressional experience and who exhibit the greatest confidence in their capacity for the divination of legislative intent through the study of legislative history.[33]

PRECEDENT

In this discussion of the arguments that the justices use to buttress their judgments, no reference has been made to precedent or, as it is sometimes called, *stare decisis.* A major by-product of the judicial system is to provide a measure of fixity, a semblance of stability, in the midst of life's changes. Changes in American society have been of revolutionary dimensions; they frequently occur with overpowering suddenness, and their ramifications are broad. Most resistant to change throughout the course of American history has been the American governmental system: our Constitution is the world's oldest, and our governmental institutions operate in the same fashion today as they did at the end of the eighteenth century. Meantime, our economic, social, cultural, and ethical systems have undergone vast change, and those of today are hardly recognizable when compared with those existing 180 years ago.

Adherence to precedent is the means whereby today's judicial decisions are related to and connected with those of the past. At judicial levels below that of the Supreme Court, literal adherence to clearly relevant precedent is more common. Run-of-the-mill litigation dominates the dockets of these lower courts. Furthermore, many lower court cases vary only incidentally with others previously decided. In such circumstances, the principle of *stare decisis* can be meaningfully applied.

The decision making of the Supreme Court is of a different kind, however. With a few exceptions, only the tough questions gain its attention, those which involve a major public policy issue with wide-ranging effects and implications. Moreover, the cases that the Court agrees to hear usually pose questions and present issues not previously resolved. Where an applicable precedent is

---

[33]Schubert, *op. cit.* fn. 15 *supra*, p. 243.

in point, the Court will either refuse to hear the matter or decide it summarily, without hearing oral argument or writing an opinion. Consequently, the principle of *stare decisis* is largely irrelevant as a guide for the Supreme Court in its decision making.

Even so, the Court's majority and minority opinions are invariably studded with references to previously decided cases. Although these references help buttress the argument contained in the opinion, they do so within the context of one or more of the constitutional or statutory bases of interpretation discussed above. Thus, a justice may find that previous Supreme Court or lower court decisions are consonant with his views of what Congress intended in the statute under review or with his interpretation of the words of the applicable provision of the Constitution. If this be so, he will cite them as the basis of his opinion.

JUDICIAL RESTRAINT

A point of view to which some justices and scholars subscribe is judicial restraint. The chief spokesman for this approach was the late Justice Frankfurter. Judicial restraint posits that judges, at least those serving lifetime appointments, are remote from popular desires and sentiments. Consequently, they should defer to those decision makers who are dependent upon popular support for their continuation in office. In the context of Supreme Court decision making, this translates to mean that judges should defer to administrative agencies and state decision makers. The rationale is that judges are much less expert about the regulated activity than are the members of such commissions as the Interstate Commerce, and Securities and Exchange Commissions; the Federal Communications, Power, and Trade Commissions; or the National Labor Relations Board. Deference should also be accorded the states by reason of the federal character of the governmental system and also because of the belief that many problems are local in character or that they are best solved at the state and local level. Such problems, therefore, should not be resolved from Washington.

Because most cases involving the federal regulatory commissions concern the interpretation of statutes, while the majority of cases involving state action concern constitutional provisions, judicial restraint, unlike the other approaches previously considered, applies to both constitutional interpretation and statutory construction. The broad category of cases most susceptible of resolution on the basis of judicial restraint are economic issues— questions pertaining to the regulation of business and labor union activities.

Analysis of decisions in which judicial restraint could have been employed shows it to be used by the justices in a consistently selective fashion: liberal justices support antibusiness and pro-union decisions of the states and the federal regulatory commissions; conservative justices, including Frankfurter, support the probusiness and antilabor decisions. This pattern is illustrated by the data in table 2 which is drawn from the first seven terms of the Warren Court (1953–1960). Douglas and Black were generally the most liberal members of the Court during this period; Frankfurter and Harlan are typical of those who were generally conservative.

Table 2. PERCENTAGE OF VOTES, BY JUSTICES, SUPPORTING MEASURES PERTAINING TO BUSINESS AND LABOR

Regulatory Areas	*Justices*			
	Frankfurter	Harlan	Black	Douglas
State action regulating:				
business	31	53	73	69
labor	91	86	10	8
Federal agencies regulating business:				
probusiness	86	83	21	14
antibusiness	35	39	95	70
National Labor Relations Board:				
pro-union	29	0	86	86
anti-union	88	67	0	0

SOURCE: Harold J. Spaeth, "The Judicial Restraint of Mr. Justice Frankfurter— Myth or Reality," *Midwest Journal of Political Science* 8 (1964), 29–36.

No distinction is made between the pro- and antilabor and business state cases because all the labor cases were decided in an anti-union fashion by the states concerned. With regard to the state business decisions, 81% were antibusiness regulations. The pattern of behavior displayed by each justice in the above table clearly indicates that judicial restraint is simply a convenient means to a liberal or conservative end. Black and Douglas support the antibusiness regulatory activity of the states, while opposing the states anti-union activities. Frankfurter and Harlan behave oppositely. At the federal level, Black and Douglas again support pro-union and antibusiness regulatory commission action, while opposing those that are not. Again, Frankfurter and Harlan display the opposite pattern.

STRICT CONSTRUCTION

A final approach which, like judicial restraint, is applied to both statutory construction and constitutional interpretation, is strict construction. It has received currency in the speeches of President Nixon about the judiciary and in his nominations of justices to the Supreme Court. However, what Nixon seems to mean by his use of strict construction is not the same as its meaning in legal circles.

In legal discussions, strict construction has two meanings. First, it refers to a literal adherence to the provisions of the Constitution. Thus, where the First Amendment says "no law" shall be made "abridging the freedom of speech, or of the press; or the rights of people peaceably to assemble," this means, according to justices such as Douglas and Black, none—period. Hence their position, previously noted, that government may not restrict freedom of speech and press because of legislative desire to outlaw obscenity and pornography. The other meaning of strict construction pertains to the interpretation of statutes, particularly in the field of criminal law. If there is any ambiguity or lack of clarity in the provisions of a law, such doubts are to be resolved in the defendant's favor. Even if we were to assume that all legislators used language with the utmost precision which, as we have noted, they do not, the multiplicity of meanings which the dictionary assigns to the average word insures some vagueness in any statute written in English.

The Warren Court, at least in its latter terms (1958–1968), appears to have adhered to the concept of strict construction. In a set of thirty-two cases concerning the construction of federal criminal statutes, the Court resolved doubt in 72% of them in favor of the defendants. Similarly, thirty-six of forty-seven obscenity decisions favored the defendants (77%), as did twenty-six of twenty-eight First Amendment decisions (93%).

Consequently, President Nixon can hardly fault the Warren Court for lack of strict construction. Given his concern for reconstituting the Court with new faces, then, Nixon must mean something different from the traditional legalistic understanding of the phrase. His concern with rising crime rates and the law-and-order posture taken by his vice-president and attorney general, as well as the Nixon Administration's espousal of a "Southern strategy," suggests that what is meant is a lessening of Supreme Court support for individual freedom and human equality—a willingness to allow the states to make their own policies in such issue areas as race relations, and a freer hand for federal and state law enforcement officials.

9

The Personal Factor in
Supreme Court Decision Making

However useful the various constitutional or statutory approaches may be, it would not be reasonable to presume that judges arrive at their decisions just because those approaches exist. The form their arguments take may well be shaped by one approach or another, but the decisions themselves are motivated by considerations more fundamental.

Based upon the assumption that all human behavior is goal oriented, and that individuals are continually faced with alternative courses of action, one may hypothesize that an individual will choose from among the alternatives available the one that he perceives best achieves his goals. The decisions an individual makes, then, will depend upon his personal value system—the set of beliefs, attitudes, and values that disposes him to behave in a certain fashion. With regard to political decision making, the relevant beliefs, attitudes, and values that motivate an individual actor's behavior may be described as his personal policy preferences.

In choosing from among alternative courses of action, an individual's personal policy preferences are not determined merely by his beliefs, attitudes, and values about the object of action *per se*. At least as important are his beliefs, attitudes, and values about the situational context in which the object of action is perceived to exist or operate.[34] Thus, an attempt to explain or predict behavior solely upon the basis of a person's attitude toward such

---

[34]Harold J. Spaeth and Douglas R. Parker, "Effects of Attitude toward Situation upon Attitude toward Object," *Journal of Psychology* 73 (1969), 173–182.

"objects" as business, labor unions, blacks, freedom of the press, criminals, students, etc. will prove to be inaccurate. Also vital to explanation and prediction is the person's attitude toward the situation: e.g., a business engaged in price fixing, a labor union striking for higher wages, blacks being bussed into the neighborhood school, the publication of pornography, criminals subject to cruel and unusual punishment, students demonstrating against administration policies, etc.

Political decision making, moreover, does not occur in a vacuum. Also affecting an individual's choice are the "rules of the game." Governing an individual's range of choice are the rule structures that specify what types of actions are permissible, those that are impermissible, and the circumstances and conditions under which choice may be exercised. These rules of the game, then, are the various structures of formal and informal rules and norms within the framework of which decisions are made. They, of course, will vary greatly from one political organization or governmental unit to another.

Among the rule structures governing the decision making of the Supreme Court are those providing access to the Court and those prescribing the procedures by which cases are to be decided. Access to the Court is limited to actual disputes between two or more persons. No federal court will decide abstract or hypothetical questions, or those in which a decision will have no practical effect. A person bringing action in the Supreme, or any other federal, Court must also have "standing." That is, an individual must have suffered, or be in imminent danger of suffering, injury to a legally protected right which the court is competent to redress.

Rules prescribing the procedures whereby cases are to be decided include the "rule of four." As noted previously, the Supreme Court has the authority to determine for itself what cases it will decide. This decision is made by four or more of the justices voting to decide to decide. Once the Court has decided to decide a case, oral argument is scheduled, after which the justices meet together to discuss how the issue or issues involved in the case shall be resolved. The chief justice states his views first, followed by the other justices in order of seniority. Upon completion of this procedure, the justices vote in reverse order of seniority. The rule governing the assignment of the opinion of the Court is, as previously discussed, that the power is vested in the senior justice who voted in the majority. With regard to the writing of opinions, these, majority as well as minority, are to be couched in legalistic, nonemotional language. They are also to pay obeisance to the rule of precedent, by justifying their judgments by extensive citation of previously decided cases.

For a number of reasons, the Supreme Court's rule structures are such that the justices are freer than other political actors to base their decisions solely upon personal policy preferences.[35] First, justices, once appointed, serve until they retire, resign, or die. Hence, unlike legislators and chief executive officers, the justices are not subject to the constraints of electoral responsibility. Furthermore, they are not subject to an effective removal power, as was noted in connection with our discussion of the selection of judges. Second, the desire for higher office is a major influence upon the behavior of most office-holders.[36] Consequently, decisions may be motivated according to their effects upon achievement of the higher office. For at least one hundred years, however, such ambition appears to have been absent from virtually every justice who sat on the Court. True, Charles Evans Hughes resigned as associate justice in 1916 to accept the Republican nomination for President. Fourteen years later, he was reappointed to the Court as chief justice. And granted, Arthur Goldberg resigned after three years' service to accept the post of ambassador to the United Nations. This appointment, however, can hardly be considered a promotion. James Byrnes, after barely a year on the Court, resigned in 1942, at President Roosevelt's request, to accept the position of Director of Economic Stabilization, a move apparently dictated by the exigencies of World War II.[37] Third, all the justices participate in all the decisions; in this

---

[35]David W. Rohde, "Strategy and Ideology: The Assignment of Majority Opinions in the U.S. Supreme Court" (Ph.D. dissertation, University of Rochester, 1971), chap. 2.

[36]Joseph A. Schlesinger, *Ambition in Politics: Political Careers in the United States* (Chicago: Rand-McNally, 1966).

sense, there is no division of labor. Finally, as the highest court in the land, the Supreme Court need not concern itself, as lower courts must, that another court may formally overrule its decisions.

The relatively non-inhibitory rule structures of the Court do not imply the absence of all constraints upon the Court's decision making.[38] They explain, rather, why the justices are less subject than other political actors to motivations other than personal policy preferences.

Ongoing analysis of the Supreme Court's decisions since the mid-1950s reveals seventy-three different categories of issues, on which the justices manifest personal policy preferences, and into which the decision making of the Court may be classified. These categories have been established by the construction of cumulative scales.[39] Cumulative scales are constructed by ordering the decisions on a given subject from 9–0 to 0–9. If the pattern that emerges is such that once a justice votes negatively as, say, the sole dissenter in a case decided 8–1, he continues to vote negatively in all succeeding cases—i.e., those decided 7–2 through 0–9 —then a valid scale has been constructed if the pattern prevails for all the justices. Figure 2 is an example of a perfect cumulative scale. Assume that the issue is an aspect of civil liberties, with the "+" votes indicating support of the civil liberties claim, and the "−" votes indicating opposition to the civil liberties claimant.

The category scales so constructed are based upon the legal and semantic content of the cases decided by the Court. As such, each category scale contains an attitude "object" and an attitude "situation." Thus, for example, the poverty law scale has "indi-

---

[37]William Howard Taft, the only person to serve both as President (1909–1913) and as a member of the Supreme Court (chief justice, 1921–1930), indicated a pronounced preference for the chief justiceship before, as well as after, his presidency. See Francis Russell, *The Shadow of Blooming Grove: Warren G. Harding in His Times* (New York: McGraw-Hill, 1968), pp. 183, 428–429, 441–442.

[38]See Thomas P. Jahnige and Sheldon Goldman, *The Federal Judicial System: Readings in Process and Behavior* (New York: Holt, Rinehart and Winston, 1968), pp. 305–357.

[39]For the methodology of constructing cumulative scales as applied to Supreme Court decision making, see Glendon Schubert, *Quantitative Analysis of Judicial Behavior* (New York: Free Press, 1959), chap. 5; and Spaeth and Peterson, *op. cit.* fn. 18 *supra*.

CASE				JUSTICES						VOTE
	A	B	C	D	E	F	G	H	I	
1	+	+	+	+	+	+	+	+	+	9–0
2	+	+	+	+	+	+	+	+	−	8–1
3	+	+	+	+	+	+	+	−	−	7–2
4	+	+	+	+	+	+	−	−	−	6–3
5	+	+	+	+	+	+	−	−	−	6–3
6	+	+	+	+	+	−	−	−	−	5–4
7	+	+	+	+	−	−	−	−	−	4–5
8	+	+	+	+	−	−	−	−	−	4–5
9	+	+	−	−	−	−	−	−	−	2–7
10	+	−	−	−	−	−	−	−	−	1–8

Figure 2: Perfect cumulative scale

gents" as its object, and "welfare benefits" as its situation. This approach ensures that every attitude object is encountered within a situational context. Hence, one is able to distinguish between indigents acting so as to secure welfare benefits from other indigents acting to secure the right to appeal from convictions for criminal offenses. Empirically, evidence shows that not all the justices respond in the same fashion to indigents in these two situational contexts. Chief Justice Warren, for example, was much more supportive of the right of an indigent to appeal his conviction then he was toward an indigent's right to receive welfare benefits. The much stronger support that the Court as a whole gave to the former type of grievance than it did to the latter is further evidence that the situational context affects the justices' behavior.

Attitude theorists generally agree that beliefs, rather than attitudes, constitute the basic psychological determinant of behavior. An attitude, consequently, may be defined as an interrelated set of beliefs about an object or situation. For social action to occur, at least two interacting attitudes, one concerning the attitude object and the other concerning the attitude situation must be activated.[40] Because of their general content, the category

---

[40]Milton Rokeach, "The Nature of Attitudes," in *International Encyclopedia of the Social Sciences* (New York: Macmillan and Free Press, 1968), I, 449–457.

scales described above are properly regarded as attitudes rather than beliefs. Compatibly with the view that "a grown person probably has tens of thousands of beliefs, hundreds of attitudes, but only dozens of values,"[41] we may define values as a set of interrelated attitudes. As such, values constitute the third and most general level of the psychological determinants of behavior.

By using the seventy-three category scales as the relevant attitudes that motivated the voting behavior of the Supreme Court justices from 1958 to 1971, we may determine the values that motivated their behavior by correlating the rank order of the justices on each pair of category scales. The resulting set of 2628 correlation coefficients (one for each pair of category scales) may be computer analyzed by a number of data reduction techniques. These techniques show that over 80% of the Court's decisions correlate together into three separate factors, dimensions, or clusters. Examination of the content of these three values indicates that they may appropriately be labeled freedom, equality, and New Dealism.

The category scales that load on the freedom dimension are those that pertain to the political and procedural guarantees of the Bill of Rights: such matters as freedom of speech, press, and association, due process, double jeopardy, and the right to counsel. The category scales that constitute equality include: voting, desegregation, poverty law, indigents, reapportionment, and protest demonstrations. New Dealism is the label used to describe the economic aspect of the category scales that load on the third dimension. These pertain to governmental regulation of business and labor: e.g., transportation, public utilities, bankruptcy, antitrust, mergers, workmen's compensation, and the rights of unions vis-à-vis management.

A justice's response to these three values, as table 3 shows, can be arranged into eight possible combinations, each of which may be considered a distinctive value system.

The description provided each value system in table 3 accords with common usage for the most part. Liberals are perceived as

---

[41] *Ibid*, p. 455.

Table 3. VALUE SYSTEMS AND VALUE RESPONSES

	Values and Responses		
Value System Description	Freedom	Equality	New Dealism
Liberal	+	+	+
Civil Libertarian	+	+	−
Individualist	+	−	−
Populist	+	−	+
Utopian Collectivist	−	+	−
Benevolent Authoritarian	−	+	+
New Dealer	−	+	−
Conservative	−	−	−

NOTE: A "+" indicates support of the value in question, a "−" nonsupport.

persons who support demands for greater political and social freedom and equality and who favor governmental regulation favorable to labor and hostile to business. Conservatives, by contrast, oppose such demands. Civil libertarians are those who focus favorably upon non-economic issues, while Individualists are the classic nineteenth–century type liberals—those who believed that that government is best which governs least. Populists are the agrarian radicals of an earlier era. Supportive of personal freedom and economic reform, they had an impact in the West and South between the 1890s and 1930s. The next two types, the Utopian Collectivists and the Benevolent Authoritarians, are most removed from the mainstream of American politics. Neither type supports freedom for their opponents, but both are high on equality. Personifying them would seem to be the various Marxist groups and supporters of the New Left, such as the student radicals of the SDS. The remaining category, the New Dealers, supports economic reform to the exclusion of personal freedom and political and social equality. Their heyday, of course, was the Great Depression of the 1930s.

In fitting the justices into the foregoing typology, the pattern shown in table 4 emerges for the fifteen justices who served on the Court between 1958 and 1971.

The pattern shows that eleven of the fifteen justices who sat between 1958 and 1971 were either liberals or conservatives, with each group almost equal in number to the other. Prior to the resignation of Chief Justice Warren, the Court was definitely

Table 4. JUSTICES AND VALUE SYSTEMS

Justices	Values and Responses			Value System
	Freedom	Equality	New Dealism	Description
Douglas	+	+	+	Liberal
Warren	+	+	+	Liberal
Goldberg	+	+	+	Liberal
Fortas	+	+	+	Liberal
Brennan	+	+	+	Liberal
Marshall	+	+	+	Liberal
Black	+	—	+	Populist
White	0	0	0	moderate
Stewart	0	0	0	moderate
Clark	—	—	+	New Dealer
Whittaker	—	—	—	Conservative
Frankfurter	—	—	—	Conservative
Harlan	—	—	—	Conservative
Blackmun	—	—	—	Conservative
Burger	—	—	—	Conservative

NOTE: A "+" indicates support of the value in question, a "—" nonsupport, and a "0" neutrality.

liberal. From the resignation of Justice Frankfurter in 1962 until the appointment of Chief Justice Burger in 1969, the Court contained only one Conservative, Justice Harlan. The Court's liberalism was especially marked in economic issues, where the liberals could expect support from Justice Clark, the last of the New Dealers, plus Justice Black. Black also associated with the liberals on freedom issues. On the other hand, the liberals commanded an absolute majority in cases concerning equality for less than two terms. Justice Fortas succeeded Goldberg, and Fortas and Marshall served together only from October 1967, when Marshall joined the Court, until May 1969, when Fortas resigned.

With Burger's accession to the chief justiceship at the start of the 1969 term, the balance of power on the Court swung to the two moderates, White and Stewart. Alone among the members of the Court, these two justices have failed either to support or oppose the three major values motivating the Court's decision making.

It should be noted, however, that the ranking of the justices in the above table is relative. Consistent voting of either White or Stewart with either the Liberal or Conservative justices could cause them—without any change in their attitudes or values—to be scored as "+" or "−". If, for example, the Court were to accept for decision cases either more liberal or more conservative in content than those it has decided heretofore, White and/or Stewart could be forced to vote sufficiently conservatively or liberally that they become aligned with either the Liberal or Conservative wing of the Court. It should also be noted that the placement of Justice Blackmun is tentative, based on his background characteristics rather than his voting behavior. In his case, however, his particular set of background characteristics indicates a high probability of Conservative behavior.

10

The Decision of the Court

The Court's decision, or judgment as it is called, is composed of two parts, the "holding" and the "disposition." The holding is the statement of the resolution of the issues presented the Court for decision, while the disposition stipulates how the case is to be handled subsequently after the Court completes its action on the case. The decision of the Court is normally located either at the very end of the opinion of the Court or follows hard upon the statement of the issues. It nearly always consists of a sentence or two. Not infrequently the holding will follow the statement of the issues or the recitation of the facts, with the disposition of the case at the end of the opinion of the Court. Thus, in *School District of Abington Township* v. *Schempp*, 374 U.S. 203 (1963), the paragraph containing the statement of the issues concludes with the holding:

In light of the history of the First Amendment and of our cases interpreting and applying its requirements, we hold that the practices at issue and the laws requiring them are unconstitutional under the Establishment Clause, as applied to the States through the Fourteenth Amendment.

At the end of the opinion of the Court is stated the disposition of the case:

. . . we affirm the judgment in No. 142. In No. 119, the judgment [of the lower court, that is] is reversed and the cause remanded to the Maryland Court of Appeals for further proceedings consistent with this opinion.

(Two separate cases were joined for decision under one opinion: the Schempp Case [No. 142] and *Murray* v. *Curlett* [No. 119]. The bracketed numbers here are docket numbers used for intra-Court administrative purposes.)

In disposing of a case, the Court will almost always either (1) affirm the judgment of the last court to have heard the case, (2) reverse that court's decision, or (3) reverse and remand the case to the lower court. The reverse-and-remand disposition is less final than a flat reversal of the lower court's decision. The remand gives the lower court an opportunity to hear further arguments and to render another decision in the case. A remand from the Supreme Court may thus provide the lower court, if it is so inclined, an opportunity to search for grounds whereby the Supreme Court's decision may be undermined. Where a case is on review to the Supreme Court from a state court, it is rare for the Court simply to reverse the state court decision. Remand here means that the state court is merely obliged to proceed in a manner not inconsistent with the holding of the Supreme Court. And if the state tribunal is determined to undo the Supreme Court's decision, it has enough discretion to accomplish that objective. The state court, for example, may find that there are new or changed circumstances in the case; perhaps the state has enacted pertinent new legislation since the case was taken to the Supreme Court; or perhaps the state tribunal may so view the Supreme Court's opinion as to allow it to declare the Supreme Court's decision as vague or unclear or to interpret it in such a way that the decision is undermined or evaded. Any one of these grounds is sufficient to allow the state tribunal to award victory to the litigant who was unsuccessful before the Supreme Court.

On the other hand, the Court has the power to order lower courts to arrive at a particular result.[42] The disposition ordered in the El Paso Natural Gas Co. Case, 376 U.S. 651 (1964), is instructive:

> Since appellees have been on notice of the antitrust charge from almost the beginning . . . we not only reverse the judgment below but direct the District Court to order divestiture without delay.

Such a particularized disposition is, however, unusual. The normal disposition of a reversed decision—of a lower federal as well

---

[42]Walter F. Murphy, *Elements of Judicial Strategy* (Chicago: University of Chicago Press, 1964), pp. 108–110.

as of a state court—is that of the Schempp Case above or of the Aptheker Case, 378 U.S. 500 (1964):

> Accordingly the judgment of the three-judge District Court is reversed and the cause remanded for proceedings in conformity with this opinion.

Of course, where the decision of the lower court is affirmed, there is no problem of compliance. The lower tribunal's decision has been vindicated; the sometimes tender sensibilities of the lower-court judges have not been affronted.

Since the Supreme Court has the authority to order a particularized disposition of the cases before it, why does it not do so more often? The answer is twofold: First, the American system of government is a federal system, one in which the component units—the states—are given a large measure of autonomy. The general intensity of feeling about "states' rights" makes a regular practice by the Supreme Court of ordering a particularized disposition in cases coming to it from various state judicial systems not only unseemly but downright dangerous to viable federal-state relations. Second, the Supreme Court has no power to enforce its decisions. Enforcement of judicial decisions rests with the executive branch of the national government. Bereft of coercive power, the Court must rely upon moral suasion. Thus it must tread softly, aiming for voluntary compliance. Its only weapon is the tradition of respect for the law; on emotionally explosive issues law and order may break down—as has been seen in the recent resistance of the South to desegregation and in the behavior of various radical political organizations. In such circumstances, the executive branch may step in, albeit reluctantly, as it did in the Little Rock school desegregation crisis of 1958.[43] But if it does not, the Court stands helpless. The ultimate safeguard of the effective functioning of the judiciary, then, is a deeply imbued respect for the law. Not only is respect for the law requisite to the functioning of the judicial system, it is also the *sine qua non* to the total operation of any truly democratic system of government.

---

[43] *Cooper* v. *Aaron*, 358 U.S. 1 (1958). Peltason, *op. cit.* fn 9 *supra*, chaps. 5–7.

Bibliographic Essay*

Probably the best brief history of the Supreme Court is Robert G. McCloskey, *The American Supreme Court* (Chicago: University of Chicago Press, 1960). A spritely account from a liberal standpoint is Fred Rodell, *Nine Men* (New York: Vintage Books, 1964). Two of the standard constitutional history texts are Alfred H. Kelly and Winfred A. Harbison, *The American Constitution: Its Origins and Development* (New York: Norton, 1955), and Carl B. Swisher, *American Constitutional Development* (Cambridge, Mass.: Houghton-Mifflin, 1954). Also see Broadus and Louise Mitchell, *A Biography of the Constitution of the United States* (New York: Oxford, 1964). Recent periods in the Court's history are treated in Alpheus T. Mason, *The Supreme Court from Taft to Warren* (New York: Norton, 1964); C. Herman Pritchett, *The Roosevelt Court* (Chicago: Quadrangle, 1969), and *Civil Liberties and the Vinson Court* (Chicago: University of Chicago Press, 1954); G. Theodore Mitau, *Decade of Decision* (New York: Scribner's, 1967); and Harold J. Spaeth, *The Warren Court* (San Francisco: Chandler, 1966). Far and away the best exposition of what the Supreme Court has said the Constitution means is C. Herman Pritchett, *The American Constitution* (New York: McGraw-Hill, 1968).

The most frequently cited source on the selection of the justices is John R. Schmidhauser, *The Supreme Court: Its Politics, Personalities, and Procedures* (New York: Holt, Rinehart and Winston, 1960). Also focusing upon the appointment of the justices is Robert Scigliano, *The Supreme Court and the Presidency* (New York: Free Press, 1971), and Joel Grossman, *Lawyers and Judges* (New York: Wiley, 1965). Case studies of single appointments may be found in David J. Danelski, *A Supreme Court Justice is Appointed* (New York: Random House, 1964), and in A. L. Todd, *Justice on Trial* (Chicago: Univ. of Chicago Press, 1964). Charles Warren's classic, *The Supeme Court in United States History* (Boston: Little, Brown, 1926),

---

*I wish to thank my colleague, David W. Rohde, and my graduate assistants, Gregory J. Rathjen and Robert Delgrosso, for their helpful suggestions.

also contains much detail about the nomination and appointment of the justices. For an incisively written account of the Senate's rejection of G. Harrold Carswell's nomination to the Supreme Court, see Richard Harris, *Decision* (New York: Dutton, 1971.)

Judicial biographies are numerous. Among the most authoritative are two by Alpheus T. Mason, *Brandeis: A Free Man's Life* (New York: Viking, 1946), and *Harlan Fiske Stone: Pillar of the Law* (New York: Viking, 1956). Other highly regarded one-volume biographies are Carl B. Swisher, *Stephen J. Field: Craftsman of the Law* (Chicago: University of Chicago Press, 1930); Charles Fairman, *Mr. Justice Miller and the Supreme Court, 1862–1890* (Cambridge: Harvard University Press 1939); and Willard L. King, *Melville Weston Fuller: Chief Justice of the United States, 1888–1910* (Chicago: University of Chicago Press, 1967). My personal favorite, because of the political treatment given the subject, is John P. Frank, *Justice Daniel Dissenting* (Cambridge: Harvard Univ. Press, 1964). Sketches of twelve of the most distinguished justices may be found in Allison Dunham and Philip B. Kurland, eds., *Mr. Justice* (Chicago: University of Chicago Press, 1964).

The best popular treatment of how the Court exercises its power is found in John P. Frank, *Marble Palace* (New York: Knopf, 1961). Illustrating the stages of the Court's decision-making process from the context of a single case is Anthony Lewis' excellent account, *Gideon's Trumpet* (New York: Vintage, 1964). Invaluable to lawyers practicing before the Supreme Court and highly informative to the layman is Robert Stern and Eugene Gressman, *Supreme Court Practice* (Washington: Bureau of National Affairs, 1962). The lower federal courts and their relations with the Supreme Court are detailed in Richard J. Richardson and Kenneth N. Vines, *The Politics of Federal Courts* (Boston: Little, Brown, 1970). Brief but eclectic is Jack W. Peltason, *Federal Courts in the Political Process* (New York: Random House, 1955). The trials and tribulations of the Southern federal district court judges in the aftermath of the school desegregation cases is provided in Jack W. Peltason, *Fifty-eight Lonely Men* (New York: Harcourt, Brace & World, 1961).

Among general studies of the judicial process is Henry J. Abraham, *The Judicial Process* (New York: Oxford, 1968). This work compares the American judicial process with those of Britain and France. Other general works include: Carl A. Auerbach, *et al.*, *The Legal Process* (San Francisco: Chandler, 1961); Lewis Mayers, *The American Legal System* (New York: Harper & Row, 1964); Glendon Schubert, *Judicial Policy-Making* (Chicago: Scott, Foresman, 1965); Stuart S. Nagel, *The Legal Process from a Behavioral Perspective* (Homewood, Ill.: Dorsey, 1969); Jay A. Sigler, *An*

Introduction to the Legal System (Homewood, Ill.: Dorsey, 1968); and Sheldon Goldman and Thomas P. Jahnige, *The Federal Courts as a Political System* (New York: Harper & Row, 1971). The best of the recent readers is Thomas P. Jahnige and Sheldon Goldman, *The Federal Judicial System* (New York: Holt, Rinehart and Winston, 1968).

Focusing upon the trial courts and their deficiencies are Jerome Frank's classic, *Courts on Trial* (New York: Atheneum, 1963); Abraham S. Blumberg, *Criminal Justice* (Chicago: Quadrangle, 1967); Howard James, *Crisis in the Courts* (New York: McKay, 1971); and James Marshall, *Law and Psychology in Conflict* (Garden City, N.Y.: Anchor, 1969).

In a category by itself is Walter F. Murphy, *Elements of Judicial Strategy* (Chicago: University of Chicago Press, 1964). This book details the ways Supreme Court justices can act to further their policy objectives.

The impact that various Supreme Court decisions have had is the subject of Theodore L. Becker, ed., *The Impact of Supreme Court Decisions* (New York: Oxford, 1969), and Stephen L. Wasby, *The Impact of the United States Supreme Court* (Homewood, Ill.: Dorsey, 1970). Related to the foregoing is John A. Garraty, ed., *Quarrels That Have Shaped the Constitution* (New York: Harper & Row, 1964), which engagingly presents the personal conflicts that produced sixteen landmark decisions in the Court's history.

Casebooks are numerous. Some cover the waterfront; others limit their scope. Among the former are Robert E. and Robert F. Cushman, *Cases in Constitutional Law* (New York: Appleton-Century-Crofts, 1968), and, for the more legally oriented, William B. Lockhart, et al., *The Ameican Constitution* (St. Paul: West, 1970). Limited in scope are Lucius J. and Twiley W. Barker, Jr., eds., *Civil Liberties and the Constitution* (Englewood Cliffs, N.J.: Prentice-Hall, 1970), and Norman Dorsen, *Discrimination and Civil Rights* (Boston: Little, Brown, 1969). Separately bound decisions, updated annually, are found in the series, "Leading Decisions of the U.S. Supreme Court" (San Francisco: Chandler). A summary of the decisions of each of the recent terms has been published annually under the title: *Decisions of the United States Supreme Court* (Rochester: Lawyers Co-operative Publishing Co.). Commentaries on the leading decisions of each of the recent terms have been published annually under the title: *The Supreme Court Review* (Chicago: University of Chicago Press). Directly involving students in the decision of actual Supreme Court freedom of speech and press cases is William I. Gorden, *Nine Men Plus* (Dubuque: Brown, 1971), an easily implemented game simulation.

The theoretical assumptions upon which coalition formation and opinion assignment may be based are found in William H. Riker, *The Theory of Political Coalitions* (New Haven: Yale Univ. Press, 1962); Robert Axelrod, *Conflict of Interest* (Chicago: Markham, 1970); Sven Groenings, et al., eds., *The Study of Coalition Behavior* (New York: Holt, Rinehart and Winston, 1970); and Albert O. Hirschman, *Exit, Voice, and Loyalty* (Cambridge: Harvard Univ. Press, 1970).

A defense of judicial restraint may be found in Wallace Mendelson, *Justices Black and Frankfurter: Conflict in the Court* (Chicago: University of Chicago Press, 1961). That the justices should be "activists" is argued in Charles L. Black, Jr., *The People and the Court* (Englewood Cliffs, N.J.: Prentice-Hall, 1960). Also see Alexander M. Bickel, *The Least Dangerous Branch* (Indianapolis: Bobbs-Merrill, 1962).

For an elementary treatment of the psychological determinants of behavior, see David Krech, et al., *Individual in Society* (New York: McGraw-Hill, 1962). A reasonably comprehensive reader is Martin Fishbein, ed., *Readings in Attitude Theory and Measurement* (New York: Wiley, 1967). Especially insightful is Milton Rokeach, *Beliefs, Attitudes, and Values* (San Francisco: Jossey-Bass, 1968). On scaling generally, see Warren S. Torgerson, *Theory and Methods of Scaling* (New York: Wiley, 1958), and Clyde H. Coombs, *A Theory of Data* (New York: Wiley, 1964). On the measurement of judicial attitudes, see Glendon Schubert, *Quantitative Analysis of Judicial Behavior* (New York: Free Press, 1959), and *The Judicial Mind* (Evanston: Northwestern Univ. Press, 1965). Also pertinent is Glendon Schubert, ed., *Judicial Decision-Making* (New York: Free Press, 1963).

A Glossary of Legal Words and Phrases Frequently Found in Supreme Court Cases

ADVISORY OPINION An opinion rendered in a hypothetical case.

AMICUS CURIAE Friend of the court. A third party who presents a brief to a court on behalf of one or the other of the parties in a case.

APPEAL A request from the losing party in a case that the decision be reviewed by a higher court. Acceptance of the request and issuance of a writ of appeal is mandatory for the higher court.

APPELLANT The party who appeals a decision from a lower to a higher court.

APPELLEE The party against whom an appeal is taken.

ARRAIGNMENT The appearance of a defendant to a criminal charge before a judge for the purpose of pleading guilty or not guilty to the indictment (q.v.).

BRIEF The written or printed argument presented to the Court by counsel.

CERTIFICATION A process whereby a lower court requests a higher court to decide certain questions present in a given case pending final decision by the lower court.

CERTIORARI A request from the losing party in a case that the decision be reviewed by a higher court. Acceptance of the request and issuance of a writ of certiorari is discretionary with the higher court.

CLASS ACTION A lawsuit brought by an individual on behalf of himself and all other persons similarly situated.

COMMON LAW Legal rules, remedies, customs, practices, and principles which are not based upon legislation, administrative regulation, constitutional provisions, or international treaties.

DECLARATORY JUDGMENT A decision of a court which declares the legal rights of the parties to the case before any injury has been suffered by either of the parties. A declaratory judgment action differs from the normal decision in that the court renders its judgment without a specific order.

DEFENDANT The party against whom legal action is taken; particularly, a person accused or convicted of a criminal offense.

DIVERSITY JURISDICTION That aspect of the jurisdiction of the federal courts which applies to suits between residents of different states.

EJUSDEM GENERIS Of the same kind. In an enumeration of certain things or conditions which also contains a catch-all phrase, the latter is limited to things or conditions of the same type as those enumerated. Thus, a listing of physical properties which contains the phrase, "and any other thing," would not be construed to apply to intangible matters.

EN BANC A decision made or a case heard by all the judges of a court.

ENTRAPMENT Inducing a person to commit a crime he had not intended for the purpose of prosecuting him.

EQUAL PROTECTION The constitutional guarantee that no person shall be unreasonably discriminated against legally.

EQUITY Legal rules, remedies, customs, practices, and principles devised by courts of law to supplement those of the common law (q.v.).

ET AL. And another; and others.

EX PARTE A hearing or examination in the presence of only one of the parties to a case, such as a writ of *habeas corpus* (q.v.).

EX REL. By or on the information of. Used in case titles to designate the person at whose instance the government or a public official is acting.

FEDERAL QUESTION A case which contains a major issue involving the United States Constitution or a provision of an Act of Congress or United States treaty. The jurisdiction of the federal courts is governed, in part, by the existence of a federal question.

FELONY A serious criminal offense, as distinct from a misdemeanor (q.v.). Typically, those crimes for which the punishment may exceed one year in jail.

HABEAS CORPUS You have the body. A writ to an official having custody of another ordering him to produce the prisoner for the purpose of allowing the court to ascertain the legality of the prisoner's detention.

IN FORMA PAUPERIS In the form of a pauper; as a poor person. Permission to bring legal action without the payment of required fees for counsel, writs, transcripts, subpoenas, and the like.

IN PERSONAM Against a person. A legal proceeding instituted to obtain decrees or judgments against a person.

IN RE In the matter of; concerning.

IN REM Against a thing. A legal proceeding instituted to obtain decrees or judgments against property.

INDICTMENT An accusation by a grand jury that a person has committed a crime.

INFORMATION A formal accusation by a public prosecutor that a person has committed a crime.

INJUNCTION A writ prohibiting an individual or organization from performing some specified action.

MANDAMUS A writ ordering an individual or organization to perform some specified action.

MISCELLANEOUS DOCKET The docket of the United States Supreme Court on which are listed all cases filed *in forma pauperis* (q.v.).

MISDEMEANOR A minor criminal offense, as distinct from a felony (q.v.).

MOOT QUESTION A case which, because of changed circumstances or conditions after the litigation was begun, no longer contains a justiciable question.

OBITER DICTA Occasionally referred to as either "obiter" or "dicta" or "dictum." An assertion made in an opinion of a court which is not pertinent to the decision made in the case.

PER CURIAM By the court. An opinion of the Court which is authored by the justices collectively.

PETITIONER The party who brings an action; the party who seeks a writ of *certiorari* (q.v.).

PLAINTIFF The party who brings an action; the complainant.

POLITICAL QUESTION Issues in a case which the Court believes should be decided by a nonjudicial unit of government.

PRIMA FACIE At first glance; without investigation or evaluation. That which, if not rebutted, is sufficient to establish a fact or case.

RATIO DECIDENDI The basis of a decision. The grounds upon which a case has been decided.

RES JUDICATA An adjudicated matter. A legal issue which has been decided by a court.

RESPONDENT The party against whom legal action is taken; the party against whom a writ of *certiorari* (q.v.) is sought.

RIGHT That which a person is entitled to keep and enjoy, and to be protected by law in its enjoyment. A right constitutes a claim when it is not in one's possession. The word "right" also signifies an interest when used in regard to property. "Right" in this sense entitles a person to hold or convey his property at pleasure.

STANDING The qualifications needed to bring legal action. These qualifications relate to the existence of a controversy in which the *plaintiff* (q.v.) himself has suffered or is about to suffer an injury to or infringement upon a legally protected *right* (q.v.) which a court is competent to redress.

STARE DECISIS To stand on what has been decided; to adhere to the decision of previous cases. It is a rule, sometimes departed from, that a point settled in a previous case becomes a precedent which should be followed in subsequent cases decided by the same court.

STAT. Statutes at large. A publication containing the public acts of Congress printed in the order of the date of each act's approval by the President.

STATUTE A legislatively enacted law.

STATUTE OF LIMITATIONS The time limit within which a legal action must be commenced.

SUB SILENTIO Under silence; without notice being taken.

SUBPOENA An order compelling a witness to appear in court for the purpose of giving testimony.

SUMMARY PROCEEDING A judicial action, usually a judgment or decision, which is taken without benefit of a formal hearing. Summary decisions of the Supreme Court are those made without the Court having heard oral argument.

TORT A willful or negligent injury to a plaintiff's person, property, or reputation.

ULTRA VIRES An action beyond the legal power or authority of a corporation, governmental agency or official.

U.S.C. United States Code. A compilation of Congressional statutes and their amendments which is organized into fifty subject titles.

U.S.C.A. United States Code Annotated. A commercially published edition of the *United States Code* (q.v.).

VENUE The jurisdiction where a case is to be heard. Normally a case is heard by the relevant court in whose district the crime or the cause of action occurred.

WRIT A formal order from a court enjoining an individual or organization to do or to refrain from some specified action.

WRIT OF ERROR A request for review of a decision by a higher court. Acceptance of the request is mandatory for the higher court. Only matters of law and not of fact are subject to review under this writ. The writ of error was abolished in 1925 as a means of bringing cases to the United States Supreme Court.

Index